ESSEX
Off the Beaten Track

Text by Stan Jarvis
Photographs by Robert Hallmann

COUNTRYSIDE
Newbury, Berk

COUNTRYSIDE BOOKS
3 Catherine Road
Newbury, Berkshire

To view our complete range of books,
please visit us at
www.countrysidebooks.co.uk

ISBN 1 85306 750 4

The front cover photograph shows Steeple
and the back cover photograph shows church ruins at Salcott-cum-Virley
The photograph on page 1 shows Hadleigh Castle

Typeset by Techniset Typesetters, Newton-le-Willows
Produced through MRM Associates Ltd., Reading
Printed in Italy

FOREWORD

C ome with me on a journey through Essex, to discover some of the places and people that have helped to shape this fascinating county of ours. In 1989, having spent some 25 years as a librarian in Chelmsford and many more years walking, cycling and motoring around this wonderful county, I wrote down my findings in a book entitled *Hidden Essex*.

The success of that book has led to this revised and updated edition, and this time it is accompanied by superb colour pictures by well-known, local landscape photographer, Robert Hallmann.

Rivers and creeks, churches and abbeys, ruined castles and windmills are all here for you to enjoy. My hope is that the pictures and stories within these pages will inspire you to seek out these treasures and help give you a better appreciation of their place in the history of this great county.

Happy travelling!

Stan Jarvis
Autumn 2002

Downham

⌘ ALRESFORD

There is a place in Hampshire called Alresford – famous for its watercress; and here in Essex there is another Alresford, noted for its Roman villa. The watercress can still be seen in any good greengrocer's, but the villa has long since been hidden by a modern house built on top of it.

The Romans must have ridden this way many a time as commuters to Colchester in the first century, when it was the premier town in England, far-flung outpost of the Roman empire. The villa was built very handily for just such a commuter, on a site very close to the present Alresford Lodge, where Alresford creek empties into the river Colne; a beautiful place to build a residence with views all down the estuary on the one hand and gently rolling woodland on the other.

It is over a century ago that C. Golding and his archaeological friends, with the permission of farmer M. H. Barton, uncovered a corridor with a tessellated floor more than 100 yards long and a room with a central, decorated floor panel some 20 ft square. Further evidence that it was Roman was found in the flue tiles of the cunningly arranged central heating system via hypocausts.

Where once the Roman officer drove his chariot to the garrison at Colchester the modern warrior of business rushes by train right through Colchester and on to London. Estates have quickly grown at Alresford to make come true the business man's dream of living in the country whilst working in the capital.

⌘ ASHINGDON

Where was the Battle of Assandune fought? It was the fight between the armies of Canute and Edmund Ironside on 18th October 1016. Canute, the Dane, had led his men on a ravaging expedition through Kent, with the subjugation of Mercia his ultimate aim. The English could not catch up with the Danes until they were on their way back through Essex. Then – was it Ashdon or Ashingdon? – Edmund at last came up with them. Battle was joined and the Danes were triumphant.

'Assandune' was identified by P. H. Reaney, the names expert, as Ashingdon, though people in the past had favoured Ashdon. The former is in the south of the county below the river Crouch and adjoining Canewdon, while Ashdon is far to the north, on the very border of the county. Herbert Tompkins, writing in 1938 was adamant: 'There are, we know, still doubting Thomases who suggest the possibility that the fight was at Ashdon near Saffron Walden, or at one of the other Ashingdons or Ashendons in England; we need not heed them.'

The present church of St Andrew, which has a nave and a chancel dated to the 14th century stands on the very site where, some four years after his victory, King Canute ordered a church to be built as a celebration of this great turning point in his life. There is not much doubt that the Roman bricks purloined by his builders were incorporated in the later church.

St Andrew's church, Ashingdon

The clock of St Andrew's commemorates the coronation of King Edward the Seventh. Instead of the numbers of the hours we see the letters of the King's name, EDWARDUS VII REX, starting at 11 o'clock. At the top the Royal Arms are emblazoned and at the bottom there is the date of Edward's death 'AD MCMX' – 1910.

⌘ AYTHORPE RODING

The picturesque mill here is a postmill, of the type which, built round a central post, is turned round to face the wind. Beneath the mill is the 'roundhouse' protecting the central post and acting as the miller's storeroom and workspace. This mill was

The windmill at Aythorpe Roding

originally built in 1779, when the land on which it stands belonged to Sir Fitzwilliam Barrington. It was completely restored and on 3rd March 1982 it was brought into the wind and about two hundredweight of wheat was soon ground into flour.

From the 15th century in the belfry beneath the broached spire of the church of the Virgin Mary the three bells have pealed:

> 'Those ancient bells in the steeple
> A million times have rung.
> Their message is clear, I am here, I am here,
> Won't you come, won't you come, won't you come?'

The man who wrote these lines was a local farmer and churchwarden for 30 years, Victor Gunn.

During the Second World War, Vic was his father's right-hand man in the family transport business, carrying goods of all kinds which were vital to the locality when fuel was rationed and supplies hard to come by. Times were hard, and Vic turned to poetry for relief; not reading it, but writing it.

With the end of the war and the nationalisation of road transport, Vic was able to see his father into retirement and, for his own family, buy Cut Elms Farm. Now he had long days on the tractor preparing the ground and harvesting the crops, time to ponder on his poetry, carrying it in his head through the long day and writing it down of an evening whilst other men would be watching television or hailing their friends in the pub or the club. Vic died in 1978, leaving as his memorial a slim paperback in which he had published eleven of his poems. There is a copy in the Chelmsford library.

⌘ BARLING

There was a time when Barling was bigger – and split into Great and Little. The Little was so small it got lost, and it is only from the air that cropmarks show where its church once stood – to the north west in the region of Bolts Farm. When it was calling people to prayer there was a quay on the river bank where boats and barges could unload.

The south wall of the parish church of All Saints proves that it was built in Norman times. The land here was owned by the King himself. It was Edward the Confessor (1042–1066) who ceded it to St Paul's cathedral. That is why some local records were lost in the Great Fire of London in 1666. There is an unusual monument here: it is a model of the windmill which stood about 200 yards north west of the church from 1763 until 1946. It started listing badly in 1903, and with the advent of steam engines the obsolete windmill was just not worth repairing. The sails were lowered to the ground in 1907; then the mill mouldered away to its eventual demolition. The model was made by Harry Manning, descendant of the last miller, Frederick Manning. After his death his widow presented it to the church for display in his memory. It was a very pleasant thought, for the mill and the church were what we might call the skyscrapers of the village, looking over it together through two centuries.

⌘ BATTLESBRIDGE

Battlesbridge is not a village in itself, it is a hamlet of Rettendon. One reason for its development was its situation on the bank of the Crouch and use of that river for transport from the earliest times. Later, a station was built here, on the Maldon and Southminster branch of what was then the London and North Eastern Railway.

A directory of 1937 shows that the Matthews, well-known as cattle and dog food manufacturers, were living at the mill house and that the mill, one of ten they

The river Crouch at Battlesbridge

owned, was in full production. Another name of note was Meeson, for William Taylor Meeson was the miller before Matthews took over.

It is interesting that the old, water-driven mill that stood astride the creek was not a river mill. The Crouch flows so slowly that it does not have the strength to turn a wheel, but there is a strong tidal flow well past Battlesbridge. So some clever fellow, whose name is now lost, built a tidal mill. It must have required many men and much effort to dam the creek with an embankment. By 1775 the mill had been rebuilt with four floors and four pairs of stones, grinding wheat into flour as fast as the barges could unload it.

The Meesons came with new ideas, they demolished the old tide mill around 1902 and turned over to steam in a new mill on the seaward side of the bridge which takes the road across the creek.

Battlesbridge is a pleasantly quiet place to visit, and very worthwhile. One can stand by the river and muse that the Crouch was a regular route for smugglers from the 18th century. They were still creeping up the Crouch as late as 1833, when the brig *Mary* was found to have tobacco and brandy worth £3,000 in the money of the day, hidden deep under its legitimate cargo of coal.

By the way, there was no battle here; the name is thought to come from the Battaile family, who were the local landowners as early as 1300.

⌘ BEAUMONT-CUM-MOZE

Beaumont Quay has crumbled away. Two hundred years ago it was busy by day and by night. During the day there was a procession of small boats and barges wending its way through the marshy maze from Hamford Water to the quay with coal from Newcastle and luxuries from London for the farmers and their families in north east Essex. At night with muffled oars the smugglers stealthily rowed in with all kinds of contraband brought across the Channel in their swift-sailing sloops. With carts and horses waiting on the wharf, smuggled goods could be in Ipswich or in London as the new day dawned.

There were few people to become curious about these dark doings; the quay was miles away from the village of Beaumont, and that was a place so small that in 1678 it was united with the even smaller parish of Moze. The parishioners pulled down the dilapidated church at Moze and carried the stone and timber over to Beaumont to repair St Leonard's church there. Once again it suffered from the ravages of time and in 1854 it was again rebuilt, to the design of architect C. Hakewill.

Beaumont Hall, a wonderful example of 17th century Essex expertise in brickwork, lies tucked away down its drive off the A136. This remarkable building replaced a much earlier house on the same site. Moze is from the Anglo-Saxon word for marsh and Domesday Book shows that out on the marshes were salt pans, three at Moze and two at Beaumont, where, when the heat of the sun was insufficient, they boiled seawater in wide pans over huge bonfires and scraped up the salty sediment. In trade then it was as good as gold.

The attractions for the traveller today include the wide views across wide fields to the marshes and the famous fishermen's seamark – the tower on the Naze.

⌘ BEELEIGH

Beeleigh is part of the parish of St Peter, Maldon. But there was a time when it was a separate little settlement carved out of the primeval forest, where bees had been so numerous that the Saxon fellers called it the 'bee clearing'.

The building which still brings significance to the name is Beeleigh Abbey, built in 1180 to house an outlier of the Premonstratensian house of White Canons at Great Parndon. The man who led them here, Robert Mantell, is shown as one of the figures decorating the south wall of All Saints church in Maldon. For over 350 years this small abbey flourished.

Beeleigh Falls at sunset

Then came the Dissolution of the Monasteries; the abbey was granted to John Gate in 1540 and nine years later he sold it to William Marche who had an extension built on to increase the living accommodation. It must have looked raw and brash at the time, but now its brick-filled timber framing so merges with the rubble stone of the abbey that the difference in age is quite forgotten. From the iron gates the appearance of these tall old buildings in a sylvan setting is a photographer's dream. During the alterations and repairs, stone coffins holding human remains were dug up under the ruins of the abbey buildings, and there has been a whisper of hidden treasure being found.

From here there is a beautiful walk past Beeleigh Grange, where the painter Sir Edwin Landseer spent many a holiday, to the meeting of the waters. The Chelmer, the Blackwater and the canal are crossed by numerous bridges as the footpath wends its way through a copse to cross the footbridge over the falls – a grand sight when the river is in flood.

⌘ BERECHURCH

Due south of Colchester's town centre is the village of Berechurch, formerly known as West Donyland. Through the centuries the place grew and separated into East and West entities. The western enclave soon took the name of Berechurch, an Anglo-Saxon appellation for a church made of boards. That church, of St Michael, is still worth a visit, dating as it does largely from the beginning of the 16th century. Within it many of the Awdeleys, or Audleys, were laid to rest. The connection of this family with Essex goes back to the 15th century, when a clever young man, born to humble parents, climbed the ladder of ambition to become the Lord Chancellor of England – and Lord Audley of Walden.

He had become Town Clerk of Colchester when he was only 28 and was a Member of Parliament at 35. Six years later he was Speaker of the House of Commons, had the ear of the King and was well on the way to fame and fortune of which his parents could never have dreamed. In the process he had to stoop to some mean acts in supporting Henry VIII's divorces, but his conscience was stilled by the large tracts of land and many buildings given him by the King. They included Walden Abbey – hence his peerage in that name. But he was not forgotten or forgiven by some people. When he died in 1544 and was buried under a grand monument in Saffron Walden church, Fuller, in his *Worthies* ... said of it, '... the marble was not blacker than the soul, nor harder than the heart, of him whose bones were laid beneath it ...'

⌘ BERNERS RODING

The Roding is the river which waters and gives its name to eight villages. Berners was the family which ruled here in the days when William the Conqueror handed out his favours. The Domesday Book of 1086 shows Hugh de Berners living at the Hall. Life for courtiers and politicians was rich but risky. Hugh's descendant Sir James Berners was still enjoying his inheritance 300 years later when he threw in his lot with Richard II, and when Richard was deposed Sir James was executed.

His daughter, Dame Juliana Berners, had been a loved and well brought up daughter, born in the country with the wide-spreading forest of Essex right on her doorstep. Little wonder, then, that she could ride and hunt and hold a hawk. It seems she enjoyed all the sports which should have been the preserve of the young lords and their squires.

As she came of age she threw off those excesses and was appointed the Prioress of Sopwell Nunnery. Here she had the time and the peaceful atmosphere in which to write. But her writings were not sacred – they were all about the very subjects which she knew so thoroughly from her youth: riding, hawking, hunting. Since this was 100 years before the invention of printing, she had to write it all in her own fair hand. When Wynkyn de Worde set up his printing press in 1491, one of the first books he produced was the *Treatyse Perteynynge to Hawkynge, Huntynge, Fyshynge, and Coot Armiris* – and it was Juliana's manuscript which formed its basis.

Today the hamlet of Berners Roding is down a tiny lane. The church is so old that its dedication has been forgotten. Juliana would have walked beside its thick old walls but her Hall has long since been rebuilt. This is a splendidly isolated place, with opportunities for walks along footpaths and bridleways.

⌘ BILLERICAY

When, in 1988, people were invited to submit the names of people and places suitable for commemoration during Essex Heritage Year, the general desire in Billericay was to mark the Chantry House as the home of Christopher Martin, the 'treasurer' of the Pilgrim Fathers. Christopher was a man of independent turn of mind in a group of people who were determined to pursue their religious beliefs. When persecution by the established church became unbearable, they moved as a group to Holland, from where Martin and two friends came back to look for a ship to take them across the Atlantic – the ship they recommended was the *Mayflower*.

They sailed it round to Leigh, took on their stores and set off round the coast of southern England in the summer of 1620, making Plymouth their last port of call. Christopher Martin, Mary his wife and his brother Solomon Prower all survived to reach the Massachusetts coast, but sadly they all died that winter during the hard life on the ship whilst they were building the colony ashore.

The proof that Christopher Martin actually lived in the Chantry House was too tenuous to satisfy the heritage plaque scheme so a substitute was suggested. This was Thomas Wood, known as 'the ghastly miller'. First he was famous for his fatness, then for his determination in dieting. He was born in 1719 and lived in the mill house on Bell Hill, looking after a pair of mills which once stood nearby.

He was a prosperous man, and showed it in his dress and in his figure. By the time he was 40 he weighed some 25 stone. But his fatness quickly took toll of his fitness: he lost his voice, he lost his teeth and was close to losing heart. A friend gave him a book all about the healthfulness of a sober and moderate diet and in a very short time Thomas became teetotal, gave up eating meat, began using dumb-bells for exercise and took a cold bath twice a week. It was reckoned that he had soon lost eleven stone in weight, and was, in his own words, 'gradually transformed from a monster to a person of moderate size'.

He lived to the age of 63 and lies with ancestors and descendants in Burstead churchyard.

⌘ BIRDBROOK

Martha Blewit as a name seems rather ordinary, yet it has a particular claim to fame, and has been remembered now for more than 300 years. Martha was the wife of the landlord of the Swan Inn and lived an uneventful life in the village, dying in 1681. She did something which very few people have done in all the years since her death – she married no less than nine husbands, to be outlived by the last. A tablet in the church tower reminds us of this fact. At her burial the priest chose as his text for the sermon, 'Last of all the woman died also'. Strangely enough there is another tablet in that same tower to the memory of Robert Hogan – who had seven wives!

As to the look of the place, there is an interesting passage in David Coller's history of Essex published in 1861: 'Of Birdbrook, which adjoins Steeple Bumpsted to the east, it was said in the last century – "In the passage from Toppesfield to this place, you are presented for upwards of half a mile with one of the finest landscapes in the county; but the pleasure received from this delightful prospect is in some measure damped upon your approach to the village, which has all the appearance of wretchedness and poverty; and indeed it is a matter of astonishment that a place so very inviting from its situation should be without one good house in it." This is a libel upon the Birdbrook of the present day. It has several neat mansions and good farm-houses; and Baythorne park, the property of Mr King Viall, standing on the acclivity above the Stour, with its park-like pastures and its fine old trees, is sufficient in itself to redeem the parish from the reproach of the surly traveller.'

The poverty of the periods of agricultural depression has gone, more professional people than ploughmen keep the houses in picturesque good order. As the writer of our day says in the district guide, '. . . as delightful a village as one could find in many a long day'.

⌘ BLACKMORE

Such goings on at Blackmore! Such parties and performances, all at the royal behest. It was, after all, such a convenient place for Henry VIII to let his hair down; only 25 miles from London, yet buried in the country. Philip Morant, the 18th century historian of Essex says that Henry, '. . . when he had a mind to be lost with his courtesans often frequented the Priory . . .' at Blackmore. It is obvious that he was doing this before the dissolution of the priory in 1525, for it was here, in 1519, that Elizabeth Blount, one of the ladies in the retinue of Catherine of Aragon, was delivered of a son. Henry acknowledged him as his son and spoiled

Blackmore's church with its 15th-century bell tower

him thoroughly, but by the time he was 17 the boy was dead. Some people say that he was poisoned by Anne Boleyn and her brother.

Henry liked Blackmore so much that he went there often, and told his courtiers he was not to be disturbed. Since the house of the former Prior of St Lawrence was known as Jericho House, enquirers were told quite simply that the king had gone to Jericho – and that phrase is now part of our language. And that is why the little stream that fed the moat which surrounded all the priory buildings was nicknamed the Jordan.

The church we see today was the priors' chapel, but it lost its chancel when it was demolished after closure of the priory. Its finest feature is the 15th century bell tower constructed entirely of huge wooden beams with timber cladding on a rubble foundation wall. Nikolaus Pevsner described it as '… one of the most impressive, if not the most impressive, of all timber towers of England'.

⌘ BLACK NOTLEY

Even today it is a small and somewhat scattered village, but it has sent at least three sons out into the wide world, to fame and fortune. Could anyone have imagined that young Bill Bedell, born here in 1571 would grow up to be a bishop? He took holy orders and became chaplain to Sir Henry Wotton, who was himself secretary to the Earl of Essex. Then, after a period as a parish priest at Bury St Edmunds, he was appointed Provost of Trinity College, Dublin, and two years later, Bishop of the two sees of Kilmore and Ardagh. He refused one of them on the principle that he could only serve one see at a time. In the 1642 rebellion, when he was already over 70, he was thrown into prison. It was only for three weeks, but the privation was such that it led to his death.

Black Notley, where the botanist John Ray was born

Richard Symonds was born in Black Notley in 1617 and took a very different course in life. He became a soldier, loyally serving Charles I as a member of his lifeguards, surviving all the important battles in the Civil War and dying at a ripe old age in the last decade of the century. He kept a notebook of points of interest in the places he visited from one battle to another and that journal is as much the reason for his fame today as his service so close to the King.

John Ray was born in 1627 to the wife of the village blacksmith. He was lucky enough to get a rudimentary education at Braintree Grammar School, which enabled him to go on to Trinity College, Cambridge. He was elected a Fellow and continued at the College for 18 years. The subject which so occupied him was natural history. Ray set himself to put in order man's recording of his natural surroundings, especially in the field of botany.

Scholars from all over the world sent specimens as he worked on his great book on plants, which was published in three volumes between 1686 and 1704 and covered some 11,000 species. His system of classification continued in use for over 200 years. He died in 1705 and was buried in the churchyard.

⌘ BOREHAM

Boreham's importance in the Saxon period is substantiated by its division at that time into six separate manors: Old Hall, New Hall, Culverts, Walkefares, Brent Hall and Porters. New Hall went on to be acquired by Henry VIII from Sir Thomas Boleyn around 1518 and he had it rebuilt as 'Beaulieu'. He was still married to Catherine of Aragon when he richly celebrated the great Feast of St George here in 1524. The Hall passed out of royal ownership in 1573, but not before it had been lived in by Queen Mary before her accession and Queen Elizabeth, who had her coat of arms carved over the entrance.

It was she who granted it to the Radcliffes, Earls of Sussex, whose grand monument is such a feature of the church. The Hall was sold by them to George Villiers, Duke of Buckingham, for £30,000 in 1620, yet, 30 years and one civil war later it went for just five shillings. Since Villiers was a Royalist, Parliament seized his estates and offered this fabulous place to Oliver Cromwell for that nominal sum. He exchanged it very soon after for Hampton Court.

The Villiers family recovered New Hall at the Restoration and sold it to General Monck, Duke of Albermarle, the man who bridged the gap between Parliamentarian and Royalist to effect the return of the Stuarts to the throne. Upon Charles II's marriage in 1661, Monck had Nell Gwynn and other court favourites come here to act *The Merry Wives of Windsor* in the vast hall of this mansion. The last royal visitor to stay here is thought to have been James II, who came in May 1686.

The Hall then experienced all sorts of vicissitudes and neglect as well as part demolition. But in 1798 it was purchased for the present owners, a community of the Regular Canonesses of the Holy Sepulchre, who established a school here. Today its reputation extends far beyond the county boundary.

⌘ BOWERS GIFFORD

Where Basildon gives way to Southend, one passes through Bowers Gifford. It joins imperceptibly with North Benfleet to the north, but it is still a lonely lane which runs south to the old centre of the village. Bowers Hall has in its grounds the remains of a moat which surrounded the old Hall. In the 13th century the Giffards, or Giffords were holding this manor by service to the mighty Hugh Bigod, Earl of Norfolk. The Giffords were related quite closely to William the Conqueror on the distaff side, so Bowers Gifford was not an unimportant place.

That knightly connection is demonstrated in the church of St Margaret, now right on the edge of the railway, so lonely, though, that it has to be kept locked. In the chancel there is a large brass, probably life-size, which was made in about 1348 to mark the grave of Sir John Gifford. It is one of the oldest of military brasses, the third oldest in the county, and it is the last brass to show armour of complete mail. Regrettably the head, part of the right leg, part of the sword and the inscription are missing. His feet are shown resting on what appears to be an amicable-looking lion.

It is amazing that it is still there today. At some time it had been removed from its site and in about 1830 it was just given away by a churchwarden. The new owner realised its worth to the parish, returned it about 1855 and, through the efforts of the Essex Archaeolgical Society it was reset again in 1898.

⌘ BRADWELL-ON-SEA

There is a place in Essex where the past meets the present in glorious solitude. Go to Bradwell-on-Sea, take the road that heads towards Eastlands, park the car and walk the half-mile or so to St Peter's chapel. You will be walking into history. This was probably the first church ever built on Essex soil. That was just after St Cedd landed here in about AD 657 on his great campaign to convert the Saxons to Christianity. The historic significance of his little church was not appreciated as the centuries passed. It was demoted to use as a kind of lighthouse, for it stands right on the sea wall; then a farmer used it as a barn, until, in 1920 it was recognised for what it was, restored and reconsecrated.

St Cedd chose a good spot for his church – the gateway of the old Roman fort, which for centuries had defied not only the raiding Norsemen but also the storming rages of the North Sea. The fort is all gone now, but that tiny church still stands there. Stroll on the beach and scuffle the sand; you will find it is not made of ground-down rock, but of millions upon millions of shells broken down by the ceaseless fretting of the waves.

Look north east and you will see the great grey bulk of the Bradwell power

St Peter's chapel, Bradwell-on-Sea

station – a brooding, gentle giant which has provided electricity since 1963. Then look back at the church – in one glance you will have covered 1,300 years!

⌘ BRENTWOOD

What chapel is more redolent of the drama of our Essex history than that old ruin of a church amidst the chrome and concrete in Brentwood High Street? We hear from time to time of people seeking sanctuary in churches and there was just such a case here in this church in 1232.

The man who sought sanctuary was Hubert de Burgh. He had acted as Regent for the young King Henry III from 1216, but when the King came of age he turned on his trusty friend and ordered his trial on trumped-up charges. Three hundred soldiers were sent to capture him. They caught up with him in Brentwood, but he dashed into the chapel and claimed sanctuary.

The soldiers laughed at the very idea. They went in there, dragged him out and took him off to London. The Bishop of London was appalled at such sacrilege. He told the King he would excommunicate him and his troops but King Henry was crafty. He knew that sanctuary could actually be claimed for 40 consecutive days only, so he deferred to the Bishop, sent Hubert back to the church, then had his soldiers surround it. Poor old Hubert gave up, and was taken off to the Tower of London and imprisonment though he was later released and died in retirement.

The ruination of the chapel had begun in 1577. Wistan Browne was Lord of the Manor and as wicked a squire as you would find in any Victorian melodrama. He claimed that this old chapel belonged to him personally and ordered his men to start knocking it down.

It was the women of Brentwood who took action. Thirty of them got together, crowded into the chapel, locked the door and threatened Browne's men with a pathetic collection of weapons which included three bows and nine arrows and two kettles full of hot water. Of course the women were soon overpowered and thrown into jail; but this disturbance came to the ears of the Privy Council. Browne was ordered to stop his desecration of the chapel and the brave women were freed.

⌘ BRIGHTLINGSEA

The view of Brightlingsea which stays in my mind is the row of beach huts stretching all along the prom – so redolent of holidays of an earlier era. As the county handbook says, 'Brightlingsea is very much a "town of the sea" for its whole life is concerned with boating and fishing'.

Its value as a port was recognised by its association with Sandwich from so early a date that even in 1442 the ceremony of allegiance then enacted was said to date 'from time immemorial'. This ceremony fell into abeyance but was re-introduced in 1888 when a deputy was chosen to represent Brightlingsea, and to pay a token sum as a remembrance of the ships and men little Brightlingsea once placed at the service of Sandwich in time of war. It is still carried out, in the belfry of the old parish church of All Saints, nearly 100 ft up, looking out on a town which migrated more and more to the riverside, so that a new church of St James was built in 1837 down where all the action was.

All Saints, a good mile away inland, was restored by a loving local band of 'Friends'. Among several points of interest is the band of tiles all round the walls of the church – each tile inscribed with the names of Brightlingsea people lost at sea, wherever in the world they might have been, from 1872 down to 1962. The first tile says, 'This record commences from the time when Arthur Pertwee became vicar of this parish'. The second tells the sad story of David Day, lost with his schooner *William* on 9th December 1872. The tile which completes the circle remembers the day in August 1962 when a man on the *Sammy* was lost overboard.

⌘ BURNHAM-ON-CROUCH

This yachting centre, patronised by the rich and the famous, is of international repute. Sailors set out from the quay to go boating on the river or to sail around the world. The Crouch is three-quarters of a mile wide here and a walk along the quayside, which stretches the length of the town itself, is fascinating and invigorating. Five yacht clubs have their headquarters here in Burham and the Burnham Week of racing and regattas is second only to Cowes.

Pubs like the Queen's Head in the little alley called Providence, and the Victoria just off the quay at the other end of the High Street offer refreshment in the convivial company of seafaring folk. Near the Queen's Head there is a small museum established by volunteers and the local history society which tells the story of the town and the general area through objects and photographs collected over the years.

Yachts at Burnham-on-Crouch

The old village of Burnham is centred on the church, which is just over a mile to the north, beside the lane which runs east to places with nostalgic names like Dammers Wick and Twizzlefoot Bridge. The church is a strong, good-looking building, but it has had its catastrophes. The tower was blown down in the great storm of 1703, the spire in 1779, and a fire damaged the roof of the nave in 1774.

⌘ CANVEY ISLAND

It took a Dutchman to drain Canvey Island when it was nothing more than the largest of a series of islands of mud and silt shifting at the whim of the Thames and the tide. A syndicate of business men approached Cornelius Vermuyden, a Dutch engineer used to fighting the invasion of the sea into his own low-lying

The Dutch Cottage Museum, Canvey Island

country. In 1623 he brought over his own team of men to embank this island, then drain it and make it fit for human habitation, with fields to be farmed.

The Dutchmen built their own houses, in their Dutch style, so that they could live on the job. Just two of them survive today. One was restored and opened in 1962 as the Dutch Cottage Museum in Canvey Road. In its two tiny rooms, one up and one down, artefacts and illustrations tell the story of this brave feat of land reclamation. The history of the island and its later development is also covered showing how good the grazing is for sheep and cattle and how the fair for their disposal was held here twice a year, with deals being done over a drink at the Lobster Smack, a charming old clap-boarded inn which claims its origin in 1563 and gets a mention by Dickens in *Great Expectations.*

Industry has largely ousted farming as the island's basic economy. People now pour in daily across the bridges to work here. The view of one end of the island is of structures, almost monumental, devoted to gas, oil and chemical engineering plants, but at the other end there is still enough solitude in the fields to encourage badgers to set up home. At the sea wall, there is a close view of the fascinating variety of shipping up and down the estuary.

⌘ CASTLE HEDINGHAM

This is a lovely little town around a triangle of streets with a fascinating variety of architecture. Take just one as an example. The Bell Inn, as a building, was put up in the second half of the 16th century on an 'L' shaped plan which has been filled in and extended, making it a rambling public house today. Its deeds show that it was in business at least as early as 1730. By 1845, it was called the Bell Commercial Inn and Posting House; the stage coach from Bury to London stopped here, bringing travellers and trade. But in the same year the trains came and the coaches made their last stop.

The church of St Nicholas has a grand Tudor tower, with a projecting stair turret under a small cupola, all in red brick. You have to go inside to see the best evidence of its building at the end of the 12th century. Look up at the amazing 'double hammerbeam' timber roof of the nave. One of only four such roofs in Essex churches, it fills one with awe and admiration of the skill of carpenters with such primitive tools.

The building above all to be visited, and open daily from the week before Easter to the end of October, is the castle. It was built in 1140 by Aubrey de Vere, son of one of William the Conqueror's leading supporters. It is one of the best preserved castle keeps in England, rising up to nearly 100 ft to the tip of its two square corner turrets. The bridge across the moat was built in 1496 to replace the original drawbridge. One of the pleasant things about a trip here is that families can enjoy the peace and quiet of these tranquil surroundings, and can picnic by the lakeside.

⌘ CHAPPEL

Chappel once had the charming name of Pontisbright. That was in the 11th century when Beorhtric, builder of the bridge (*pons* in Latin), or owner of the land, was probably still remembered with gratitude for providing a bridge over the Colne where formerly pedestrians had to wade a risky ford. It was in those days that a chapel was built here for the convenience of the growing number of worshippers who could not get across to Wakes Colne church when the river was in full flood after rain or snow.

The architect of the other bridge which crosses the river, the magnificent railway viaduct, is not remembered locally in any way at all. Yet this viaduct of 30 arches required some 7,000,000 bricks to carry the railway that essential 320 yards. It was the largest viaduct the Great Eastern Railway ever built and still holds the record as the biggest in East Anglia. Such a huge construction must have been a great blot on the landscape when it was first put up in 1849 but its presence is now accepted as a mellowed feature, which all can enjoy by means of a circular amble of two miles. The walk returns you to the green, overlooked by houses in attractive architectural variety beside the church of St Barnabas. The thick stone walls of that church were raised back in 1352 and the building has been kept in repair ever since.

If, on viewing the viaduct you feel a bit nostalgic for the sound of steam and the smell of smoke, just cross the river to the old Chappel and Wakes Colne station. It has been practically reconstructed, to look as it did when the Marks Tey, Sudbury and Bury Branch line and the Colne Valley Railway took folk on to the main line to London and the coast. Old locomotives and carriages which match them in age and atmosphere revive memories of smuts in the eye on Sunday School outings.

⌘ CHELMSFORD

There are few corners of the county town which have stayed hidden from the prying eye of the developer through the last century. Those buildings which have survived, like the Shire Hall and the cathedral have been well covered in guide books. But there is a monument to Victorian engineering which does get overlooked. Citizens see the brick piers and the high arches of the railway viaduct striding across river and road as something of an eyesore. However, the sheer daring and the brilliant engineering of these railway pioneers is being recognised and stations, bridges and viaducts are being seen as examples of industrial archaeology, to be preserved for the insight they give us into that great age of steam.

When one considers the oozing, yielding clay of the meadows where the Can and Chelmer flow it is something of a miracle that the viaduct has stood firm for nearly 160 years. The architect made it as graceful as he could with the material he had to use – bricks, millions of them. The *Essex Chronicle* of 3rd March 1843 tells of the first 'Trip throughout the line' by a party of 20 men responsible for financing

The Chelmsford viaduct

and laying the railway: '... After emerging from the cutting, a prominent feature of the works, the Cann viaduct presented itself – as fine a specimen of a work of the kind as is to be found upon any line in the kingdom. It consists of 18 arches, each of them of 30 ft span, and 44 ft in height, with massive wings to sustain the embankment at each end. Topped with a light and elegant iron parapet which is now in the course of erection, it forms a beautiful and picturesque object when viewed from the New London Road. A short embankment connects this with the Chelmsford viaduct, and in the erection of the two structures 10,400,000 bricks have been laid.

'The Chelmsford viaduct is a masterpiece in this department of railway works. The construction is of a peculiar nature, being a double line of arches, extending upwards of 800 ft ... The station, as we have before stated, is a neat, elegant and light structure of timber, in which every accommodation is afforded for the public and the officers.'

We take travel by train so much for granted today that it is difficult to appreciate the great excitement occasioned by that first trip, graphically described in the same newspaper: 'About half past twelve o'clock the shrill whistle of the fiery visitant, and the rumble of the train which he so steadily bore up to the station, turned many a wondering eye in Chelmsford in that direction, and soon parties began to trip thitherward, to the desertion of the fireside or shop, and the emptying of mine hosts' inviting benches, to indulge in a little speculative curiosity on the snorting stranger ...'

⌘ COLCHESTER

Holly Trees, the big, old house which shelters Colchester's museum of 'bygones' has a strange connection with the lost village of Markshall and with the church at

The Holly Trees Museum, Colchester

Coggeshall. If you look outside, up against the creeper-covered side wall stands a row of tombstones. Decipher what you can and you will find that they all refer to a Honywood family.

Mrs Honywood was married when she was 16 years old, had 16 children and came to live in Essex in 1605 as a widow aged 77. She came here because her son Robert, then living in Kent, needed a bigger house for his family of 15 children, and he found just what he wanted in the Hall at Markshall – a hamlet on the road from Coggeshall to Earls Colne. A good son, he took his mother along with that big family and she lived happily with them until her death at the age of 93.

Meanwhile her other children were being just as fruitful as Robert. In fact Mrs Honywood's 16 children produced so many more children in their turn, who also had large families, that, even while she was still alive that grand old lady could claim 367 descendants. But life has hurried on; not just the Hall but the church and its yard, where so many of the family were buried, have disappeared.

When the church was torn down in 1933 the tombstones and monuments to various members of the Honywood family had to be disposed of. Heads were scratched and a compromise was agreed. All the family stones which could be recovered were to go to the museum, even though they have to stand outside, but the very special monument to Mrs Honywood herself was 'taken in' as it were, by Coggeshall church. It can still be seen there on the wall of the sacristy – a small reminder of a big family.

⌘ COPFORD

The parish fronts the old A12 trunk road (now the B1408) from Marks Tey to Stanway. Houses line the road because in the days of coaches and horses there was plenty of trade with the travellers to enrich the inhabitants. On the north side of the road, the windmill, a post mill, stood on its little hill. Robert Oliver was the miller down to 1733; then it changed hands several times before the Ely family took it on through most of the 19th century. In a terrific thunderstorm in July 1859 the mill was struck by lightning and extensively damaged. By 1900 nothing was left but the rotting, weatherboarded body, which was shortly afterwards completely demolished, and later even its mound was levelled. Only the name of the inn, the Windmill, recalls that monument of village self-sufficiency.

The centre of Copford is much further south, where Copford Hall and the parish church stand in peaceful partnership. Travellers come from all over the world to see the remarkable architecture of the church of St Mary the Virgin and its wonderful wall paintings.

The only additions to the original 12th century building are a south aisle added in the 14th century and a bell turret possibly 100 years after that. For some reason now unknown, the stone vaulting of the nave and chancel was removed and replaced by timberwork. The wall paintings are an astonishing survival, for they were part of the original decoration.

⌘ CRANHAM

This is a place of change. It has changed its name; in the distant past it was called Bishop's Ockendon because it was that part of old Ockendon owned by the Bishop of London. It has changed its church; the old one became so ruinous that it had to be demolished and the new All Saints rose on the old site in 1874. The Hall has also been rebuilt since the days when General James Oglethorpe lived there and worshipped at the church. He is Cranham's most famous son, though he was actually born in Godalming. He became Member of Parliament for Haslemere and through 32 years as an MP campaigned for prison reform. One way out for the poor prisoner of those days was settlement in the colonies. Oglethorpe led an expedition to Georgia in 1732 and put in hand the building of the settlement of Savannah. While he was there the Spanish attacked Georgia during the War of Jenkin's Ear of 1739. Oglethorpe commanded the defence and routed them at the Battle of the Bloody Marsh. Although he remained Governor of Georgia until 1752, he came back to England in 1743, and at 47 years of age courted and won Elizabeth Wright. She was a young heiress, who on her parents' deaths had come into Cranham Hall and Canewdon Hall estates. After a couple more years in Parliament, Oglethorpe retired, and for 30 years lived peacefully with his wife on their estate, riding out over the fields and entertaining famous people of the day like Walpole, Goldsmith and Boswell who were his intimate friends, until his death in 1785. A plaque in the parish church marks his last resting place.

⌘ CREEKSEA

Of all the characters who enlivened life in Essex in the second half of the 18th century, Sir Henry Bate-Dudley was one of the most colourful. He lived at Bradwell Lodge. He was parson, magistrate, sportsman, farmer and editor of a national newspaper, and also an enthusiastic huntsman, who had the strange distinction of being the only one ever to have been in at the kill on the roof of a church.

It happened like this: following his own pack of hounds, he left his fellow huntsmen far behind as the fox ran and ran. It ended up in the churchyard of All Saints at Creeksea, where it scrambled up an ivy-covered buttress, looking for sanctuary. A couple of hounds also made the perilous climb. Not to be outdone Bate-Dudley hauled himself up after them, and as his friends wearily straggled in he swore that he had been in at the kill right there on the roof of the chancel.

He died in 1824, aged 79, by which time All Saints was going into a decline. It was rebuilt in 1878 in stone of various hues, in a romantic village church style very typical of Frederick Chancellor, the Chelmsford architect who achieved a greater place in Essex history by becoming the first Mayor of Chelmsford. Look carefully and you can see that some of the Norman zig-zag decoration of the old church has been incorporated in the wall of the new.

⌘ DANBURY

Danbury Palace was once the home of a bishop, and during the last war it was a maternity home. Long, long ago there was no house there at all; it was the deer park belonging to St Clere's Hall on the other side of the road. King Henry VIII granted it all to his brother-in-law William Parr, and he sold it straight away to the local squire, Sir Walter Mildmay.

Danbury church in winter

He it was who built the first house here and called it Danbury Place. Sir Humphrey Mildmay, born in 1593, lived here in great style. But he backed the Royalists in the Civil War, so he had to lie low through the Commonwealth period. He stayed at home, drinking and gambling with the rector, Clement Vincent, who had been thrown out of the living by the Puritans. They also seized Mildmay's lands and he had to pay more than £1,000 to get them back.

After his death, Danbury Place passed through several hands and the estate was split up, until the dilapidated old house was reduced to the status of a mere farmhouse. Then John Round bought it, in 1831, pulled it all down and built the present house. He employed the famous architect Thomas Hopper, but his wife Susan also had a lot to do with the design, ensuring that three staircases were installed, one of them entirely of stone, for she had a great fear of being trapped in a fire.

Poor woman, she did die in a fire, in a London hotel. John Round brought her body back to lie in a grave in Danbury churchyard, which is still marked. He could not bear to live in the house without her and put it up for sale in 1845. It was bought by the church to serve as the Palace for the Bishop of Rochester, whose diocese then included Essex. A beautiful chapel was built on to the Palace. Then the diocese boundaries were revised, Essex was excluded, the Bishop moved and the Palace was sold in 1892.

The beautiful lakes which formed part of the early gardens are now in the public domain.

⌘ DEDHAM

This is a great place for a day out, with historical associations to look up, architectural beauty to look at and countryside so inspiring that it has been captured on canvas by one of our greatest English painters.

John Constable crossed the Stour every day to come to school in Dedham. Looking back in adulthood he said, 'I love every stile and stump, and every lane in the village . . .' He expressed that love in paintings like Dedham Vale and Dedham Lock which, in countless reproductions, are proudly hung on walls of houses all around the world.

We can walk in his footsteps down to the lock. The mill on the Stour here is now a block of prestigious flats, but the water meadows are still there, where we can wander, and recharge our spiritual batteries just as Constable did.

The church, a real beauty, was built through the piety of merchants made rich in the cloth industry, which was thriving in Essex in the 15th century. By the time the whole church was built, over 30 years from 1492, the woollen trade was declining. So, just in time, St Mary's was built, and has been kept in repair for us to appreciate 500 years later.

The house opposite, Shermans, is owned by the National Trust. It sports an

The river Stour, near Dedham

unusual sundial high up in the centre of the parapet, but this is just one feature of its early Georgian facade. There are many other interesting old houses on the way through the town to the toy museum, which shows objects from round the world and down the ages.

Last, but not least, at Castle House the studio of the artist, Sir Alfred Munnings, is kept just as it was when he was at the height of his power. He, like Constable, found inspiration in the beauty of Dedham and its environs.

⌘ DOWNHAM

Downham is not recorded in the Domesday Book under that name. It first appears as 'Dunham' in the Red Book of the Exchequer of 1168, and as Dounham in property deeds from the 13th century, when Barn Hall is mentioned.

In the next century we can read of another property, belonging to the de Hemenhale family, which was still called Fremnells 600 years later when the water in the Hanningfield reservoir slowly rose to obliterate all evidence of its existence. It was held, as the Manor of Hemnales, by Sir Thomas Tyrell up to his death in 1476. In 1683 Sir Thomas Raymond died in possession of it and was buried under an altar tomb in the church. Two centuries later the manor house was described in a sale catalogue as: 'An ancient MANSION, now occupied as a Farm House'. By 1937 Fremnells had resumed its status as a nice place in the country, lived in then by a local Justice of the Peace, Lawrence Kirk.

In 1954 Nikolaus Pevsner, writing in his *Buildings of England* series, states that the house as he saw it dated from about 1630. It had those stone-mullioned windows which make an English country house so handsome. He concludes 'It is said that the house is to be submerged by the Hanningfield reservoir. That would be a thousand pities, as it is the best house of its day in Essex'. A footnote to the 1965 edition simply says, 'It has been submerged'.

It must be said that since the Hanningfield scheme, completed in 1956, the 354 hectares of the reservoir have the beauty of a lake, with marginal lands planted with conifers and hardwoods. Birds and butterflies are attracted, wild flowers have crept back and one section is a bird sanctuary.

⌘ EARLS COLNE

Earles Colne is a pleasant place in which to live, as witnessed by the number of fine houses which can be seen here.

One of them is Colne House; its story began with Mary Gee who by 1837 was left widowed and childless. She was rich and had already used her money to benefit the locality: she had backed the setting up of a charity school in Great Maplestead in about 1836 and she provided a purpose-built, village school there in 1863. In 1838 she had founded an infants school in Earls Colne itself.

At the same time she put in hand the building of a new house for herself. It was to be called Colne House, and it was ready for occupation by 1840. She lived here with her companion, Elizabeth Barter, the schoolmistress of her school, until she died on Christmas Eve 1864. By then her benefactions had also included more than two thirds of the cost of building the church of the Holy Trinity at Halstead and the whole cost of erecting St James at Greenstead Green in 1845.

Her nephew, Lt. Col. Frederick Marsden then occupied Colne House. Then it changed hands several times until 1946, when it was bought by Arthur Evans. Prior to the Second World War he had written to Winston Churchill, pointing out the Germans' virtual monopoly in the manufacture of photocells and the problems it might cause if war broke out. Churchill's reply encouraged Arthur Evans to do something about it himself. He set up Evans Electroselenium and by the time war did come he was exporting photocells in competition with the Germans.

The parish church, Earls Colne

As to the house, he made a number of tasteful improvements and restored the garden from what had degenerated into wartime potato patches.

Half a dozen houses in Earls Colne could be chronicled in this manner, with the school and the church yet to be mentioned! The church was much restored in 1884, but the windows in the south aisle prove its origin in the 14th century. The story of Earls Colne Grammar School has been comprehensively told by A. D. Merson in his history published by the governors of the school in 1975.

⌘ EAST HANNINGFIELD

What satisfaction there must be in digging for water and eventually finding it. The idea of having water on your land was just a dream to most villagers in the 18th century. Even the parson at East Hanningfield did not have this useful perquisite until he set the work in hand himself – and what an arduous task it turned out to be. A reader, writing to *The Gentleman's Magazine* on 8th July 1791 reported:

'It was begun June 21, 1790, and water, when the workmen, from such tedious labour, were at the moment of despair, was found May 7, 1791. Thirty-nine thousand five hundred bricks were used, without cement, in lining this well, the soil of which ... was a fine, light-brown, imperfect marl ... [which] continued to 450 feet, where it was consolidated into so rocky a substance as to require the being broken through with the mattock. A bore then, of 3 inches diameter and 15 feet in length, was tried, which soon, through a soft soil, slipped from the workman's hands and fell up to the handle. Water instantly appeared, and rose within the first hour 150 feet, and, after a very gradual rise, now stands at 347 feet, extremely soft and well-flavoured ...'

The parson had dug the well for the benefit of his parishioners, 'for whose use it is always open' he declared.

They benefited from water – but suffered by fire; the church was burnt down on 5th January 1884. That fire brought to light under coats of lime wash some exquisite wall paintings done around AD 1300. The vicar tried to protect them behind glazed doors, but vandals broke them. In 1933 one portion of these paintings was successfully peeled from the wall for preservation in the Victoria and Albert Museum.

The church we now see was built in record time; started on 16th July 1884, it was consecrated on 16th June 1885.

⌘ EPPING

Epping grew up as a settlement in the forest – a first or last stop on the way to and from London. The forest shrank back from Epping as it was used for building timber and for fuel by the growing town, but it was still the place for jolly jaunts out from smoky, crowded London. In 1830 Thomas Hood, the celebrated poet and humorist, tells of the famous Epping Easter Chase.

'I attended the last Anniversary of the festival, and am concerned to say that the sport does not improve, but appears an ebbing as well as an Epping custom ...'

The hunt Hood describes was a comical, noisy disaster. Today more sober expeditions can be made to savour historical sites in close proximity to Epping. A mile out of town on the B1393 (formerly the A11) is a banked enclosure by the road on the left-hand side opposite the lane to Upshire. This is Ambresbury Banks. Some historians believe that behind this inadequate rampart Boadicea, or Boudicca, and her faithful British tribesmen took up their last stand against the might of the Roman army in AD 62 and were annihilated.

Copped Hall is best approached on foot along a path from that lane to Upshire. Along a hedgerow with beautiful views to the east, the path is carried over the M25

The ruins of Copped Hall, Epping Forest

on a bridge. The walk is the most important part of the visit, for the Hall is now a roofless ruin, destroyed in a terrible fire in 1917. Its beauty of white brick against the verdant woods and before the rippled lake is gone but there is a lingering atmosphere of the famous and the wealthy who called this place home from its building in 1753. Long before that there was a house on this site. Princess Mary, later Queen Mary I was living here in 1551 when the Privy Council ordered that she should cease having the Roman Catholic mass celebrated here.

⌘ FAULKBOURNE

The spot I like best, largely for its place in the legendary history of Faulkbourne, is the pond at the edge of the road between Home Farm and the church. Though not shown on the map, this is a pond of great significance, for it is fed by a spring which was in the earliest times considered a holy well, long before the Saxons were converted to Christianity. It is most likely that the present church was sited on this spot because it was the accredited holy place of the pagan gods.

The spring was thought to have healing powers which attracted pilgrims. It was called St German's Well and the church is dedicated to the same missionary bishop. In it one can trace through the architecture of the nave and the chancel, its origin in Norman times. The Hall, which stands close by, has been declared the finest 15th century mansion now existing in the county, carried out in warm, red brick, even to its towers, turrets and battlements.

Look out for the old former post office just a little further up the street. Notice under the bedroom window a small shutter, still in position after 200 years. It was fixed there by an enterprising postmaster. When the Witham mail coach came clattering through the village on an early winter's morning the poor old postmaster had to creep downstairs in his nightshirt and open his door to frost and snow as he took in the mail for the village. Since mail coaches were pretty tall affairs the postmaster built this little hatch through the wall beside his bed. The coachman had only to tap on it with his whip and the postmaster could open it, take in his letters and still stay snug and warm!

⌘ FELSTED

A small enough place, but it has certainly left footprints in history. The first one relates to the Domesday Book and shows us that the Normans were as fond of a joke as we are. To appreciate their joke you should first look in the telephone directory under the name Godsalve, Godsave or Godsafe. You'll see a lot of entries of a family name which goes all the way back to that Domesday Book. It sounds a very pious name – but look under Felsted in that book and you will see that the King had given land there to one of his knights, recorded as 'Roger God-save-the-ladies'! It is not surprising, then, that he had quite a few descendants!

Four hundred years later and the second footprint is the amazing monument in the church under which lies buried Richard Rich. He was born in 1500; by the time he was 48 he had become Lord Chancellor and was handling vast sums of money on behalf of the King in the acquisition and resale of monastic property. He obtained Leez Priory for himself and so came to live in Essex. For another 20 years he kept his head while those about him were losing theirs, serving a succession of sovereigns and retiring to Leez. He had a number of estates in Essex and died at one of them, Rochford Hall.

It was he who founded Felsted school in 1564, so it is not unreasonable that he should choose this church in which to be buried. Yet his grand monument had to wait until around 1620, when his grandson put in hand a magnificent memorial in multi-coloured marbles, showing Lord Rich with his son, who died in 1581, backed

The memorial to Lord Rich in Holy Cross church, Felsted

by a group of figures in high relief representing Wisdom, Truth, Justice, Fortitude, Hope and Charity, under a canopy supported by two bronze columns. The work is probably by the famous Epiphanius Evesham.

For all the grandeur of that tomb there was a humble craftsman whose name is more immediately in the public eye. Look along the bressumer, the main horizontal beam supporting the upper floor of the house opposite Lord Rich's original school and you can read the message, 'George Boot made this house, 1596'. Wouldn't he be proud to think that it was standing still, after 400 years?

⌘ FINCHINGFIELD

In every Essex calendar you buy there is always a shot of the pond at Finchingfield and the steep hill beyond it leading up to the church. It is such a picturesque place, what with the timber-framed Guildhall, under which one passes to the church with its sturdy Norman tower, and the old windmill just around the corner.

Look for Spains Hall, down the side road, when it offers an open day in aid of charity. William Kempe was born here in 1555, had a happy childhood, married and saw his daughter happily married while he stayed here in Spains Hall. One day, in the course of a silly tiff, he accused his wife of being unfaithful. He knew she never had been, and he regretted his words so much that he there and then

Finchingfield, the 'Calendar Queen of Essex'

made a vow that he would not speak again for seven years. Folklore has it that for every year that passed he had a large fishpond dug out in his garden. Even when his wife died in 1623, he kept his vow of silence. It is said that, in 1628, at the end of his seven years of silence he tried to speak again, and found he could not utter a sound. The shock killed him! You can read his memorial in the south aisle of the church.

⌘ GESTINGTHORPE

In the tower, added to the Norman church of St Mary around 1498 there is a message; with hindsight, a message of sadness and regret. The fifth and sixth bells are inscribed: 'In gratitude to God for the safe return with honour of my beloved son from the dangers of war in South Africa'.

That son was Lawrence Edward Grace Oates. He grew up in Over Hall, better known today as Gestingthorpe Hall, in the 1880s. He was a frail boy, but age brought strength and at 20 years old he was a subaltern with the Inniskilling Dragoons. In December 1900 he stepped ashore in Cape Town and was immediately sent into action against the Boers. His bravery earned promotion to Lieutenant, and subsequent daring feats in action earned him the nickname 'No surrender Oates'. After a particularly bad injury he returned to Gestingthorpe to convalesce – the reason for the inscription on the bells.

Oates then got special leave from his regiment to join Captain Robert F. Scott in his attempt to reach the South Pole. By 16th January 1912 they were just 27 miles short of the Pole. They saw the tracks which showed them that Amundsen had beaten them to it; nevertheless they struggled on to the Pole. On the fearful fight back to their base camp Oates became desperately ill. He knew he was holding back the small band's attempt to reach safety. He purposely walked out of the tent into a blizzard saying, 'I am just going outside, I may be some time'. Of course he never came back. There is a brass on the north wall of the church which records this last act of bravery. The visitor who reads it can look up to a nave roof erected 500 years ago of a double-hammerbeam construction – complicated, beautiful and rare in our county.

The Hall, built in the 18th century is still there.

⌘ GOOD EASTER

The eminent local historian Philip Dickinson writes, 'Good Easter, one might say, is very "Essex" in appearance and its distinctive wooden tower and spire, though modern, rising from within the west end of the nave, is reminiscent of many others in the county where building stone is non-existent and wood and flint form the only alternatives'. The church was the subject of a dreadful fire on 22nd March 1885, which destroyed both the old tower and the nave. From Philip Dickinson we also get the explanation of why the south doorway of a parish church so often has a

St Andrew's church, Good Easter

porch. At Good Easter it was added in the 15th century. In those days the first part of the marriage service was performed outside the church in the presence of witnesses – a legal necessity before written confirmation in the church register was introduced.

The chancel of St Andrew's, which survived the fire unscathed, is long and narrow, built of flint around 1200 and lengthened within the next 30 years. The Victorian tower and spire rise to a combined height of 109 ft.

Many timber-framed houses, and at least eight moated homestead sites still grace the gently rolling landscape. That it was farmed in Saxon times is evident from its name, which can be loosely translated as 'Gōdgifu's sheepfold'. Gōdgifu has been identified as the widow of a Saxon earl who bequeathed all her land to the monastery at Ely.

⌘ GRAYS THURROCK

Grays Thurrock, named after Richard de Grays, who was granted Thurrock Manor in the 12th century by Richard Coeur de Lion, had a great advantage – a long frontage to the Thames, down which its fishermen sailed to the estuary and the fish-full North Sea. Crops of all kinds brought by boat and barge round the coast from East Anglia were unloaded here to feed the growing population. But most of all, in later years it was the loading-place for the bricks made in their millions in Grays – bricks which built the ever-spreading London suburbs, the viaducts and bridges which carried the railways out of the capital and so killed the riverborne trade. An old photograph of the brickfield at Hogg Lane in 1910 shows a vast sea of bricks, stacked in rows which stretch away into the distance.

One owner of much of the Thames-side property in the 17th century was William Palmer. He was Lord of the Manor, married twice but died childless in 1710. He left a legacy to have Palmer's School built opposite the parish church where it stayed until 1871. It continues still in Chadwell Road as Palmer's Sixth Form College. But for all his long-lived endowment, and his importance in his time, nobody knows where he was buried – no tomb, no monument, not even an entry in a burial register has been found.

⌘ GREAT BARDFIELD

At the height of its importance it was a town with a busy market, but since its market cross was removed around 1769 you can tell it was a long time ago.

The old 'town hall' was built in 1859 in a style more reminiscent of a chapel, hidden now by pollarded limes. Further along the street is the Cottage Museum opened in 1961 in a restored almshouse. In a small space a varied collection of local 'finds' and the implements of an earlier generation rub shoulders with a remarkable collection of corn dollies.

The old village green, outlined by a triangle of roads, has been entirely built upon, except for the little graveyard of the Friends' Meeting House. It must be said that the architecture, gloriously muddled in period, is just as attractive to the visitor's eye as a triangle of close-mown grass.

Bridge End, down by the Pant, or Blackwater has changed drastically over the last 30 years. Old cottages have been swept away and the opportunity has been taken to open up new, interesting vistas. Great Bardfield certainly is a place in which to walk about, even as far as the old windmill, Gibraltar Mill, now a private house, and down the lane beside it to the watermill, with the cool sound of water splashing into the pool. Footpaths run on, up and down the riverbanks, inviting one to stroll just that little bit further.

The windmill at Great Bardfield, now a private house

⌘ GREAT BRAXTED

Braxted Park is a mansion originally built for the D'Arcy family. It was much rebuilt and extended to the form we see today by Peter Du Cane and his grandson, also Peter du Cane, who by 1834 had not only altered the house considerably but also enlarged the park by adding the neighbouring estates of Fabians and Pundicts. In 1833 the grandson Peter took over the rectory and its glebeland, building a new rectory in 66 acres of land.

There was just one problem, the whole village of Great Braxted stood within the shadow of the church and within the Du Cane's park. Du Cane simply offered to rehouse all the people further south at Bung Row, in new houses; they agreed, all the old houses were pulled down and the squire set about building a wall around his park. He started it at the entrance by the Kelvedon Lodge in 1825, and worked all the way round. At the end of each year's completed work he had a stone placed in the wall carrying his initials and the year. That wall is still there today and it is no less than four and a half miles in circumference.

He had an icehouse in the park, built in the 18th century, with just a round hole for access. It was said by the locals that he offered £100 to any man who would live in it for a whole year without shaving or washing. Food, drink and tobacco were to be abundantly available. One man took him up – and was £100 richer at the end of the year. Ever after that it was known as 'The Hermit's Cave'.

⌘ GREAT BURSTEAD

On the night of 23rd/24th September 1916, Zeppelin L32 crossed the Channel with orders to bomb London. Lieutenant Sowrey had taken off from Hornchurch aerodrome in his frail aeroplane to deter it and the rest of the Zeppelin fleet. He found the L32 and went into the attack.

The Zeppelin was soon in flames and fell slowly to earth in an appalling fireball, so bright that people 20 miles away could see clearly enough to read a newspaper. It crashed down in meadows about one mile east of Great Burstead's houses. No survivors were found. By four in the morning the crowd was gathering and Londoners from 25 miles away streamed in all through the day.

By mid-morning hundreds of soldiers had formed a tight circle which extended all round the smoking remains 250 yards long and 25 yards wide, to keep back the enormous crowd. The searchers recovered 28 bodies of German airmen and on 27th September they were buried with no publicity in Great Burstead churchyard. For a long time after the war, wreaths were sent from Germany to be placed upon the graves but in the 1960s the remains were exhumed and sent to the German war cemetery in Wales, for the convenience of German visitors.

⌘ GREAT HALLINGBURY

People often complain of the damage done to churches by the over-zealous 'restoration' of well-meaning Victorians. This church demonstrates what one Victorian did to modernise a church. 'John Archer Houblon wished to make the church sound and in every way fit for worship by his neighbours, tenants and his employees. He therefore repaired and enlarged; and in both he swept away – with a cold logic like that of a design engineer.' That is how Heather Cocks and Colin Hardie put it when writing the booklet issued in 1974 to commemorate the centenary of that drastic restoration.

The monuments and memorials which had accumulated in the main body of the church were taken down and placed all together in a room below the tower where all their details can be read, while the pure uncluttered lines of the interior architecture can now be appreciated. As to the exterior, Mr Houblon used old material to extend the north aisle so that the enlargement matched the existing fabric. He rebuilt the spire as a replica of a former one which had been destroyed by lightning in 1738. He died in 1891, aged 88, having been a good 'squire'. Tangible evidence is the memorial he paid for at Anvil Cross in memory of a villager struck by lightning there, and the school he paid for in 1851.

His house, Hallingbury Place, was built by his forebears on the site of the mansion in which Henry, 11th Lord Morley entertained Queen Elizabeth in 1561 and again in 1576.

⌘ GREAT SALING

You certainly need a map to find your way to Andrews Field aerodrome, just behind the village. This was the first aerodrome to be built by the Americans in this country. They came in July 1942, finished the job in under one back-breaking year and named it after one of the famous generals in their air force, Frank M. Andrews. The hard core for the runways came from the ruins of the London blitz and the speed of construction was achieved by two shifts of men working flat out through 24 hours a day.

From it flew the Flying Fortresses, then Marauders and, towards the end of the war our own Spitfires took off to meet the challenge of the 'doodlebug' and the rocket. There are little landmarks which catch the imagination, like the lump of concrete by the old main entrance in which, when it was still wet, a GI had scrawled: 'Johnny Caruso, Brooklyn, New York, 24th April 1943'. Back in the village, close by the White Hart, read the inscription on the memorial, fashioned in the form of a large bird-bath in a little roadside garden with benches where the visitor can rest and wonder at the courage and tenacity of that generation. The inscription ends:

'The warmth and generosity of the British people in this community has not been forgotten. This marker is dedicated to these friends and to our comrades who later made the ultimate sacrifice in western Europe. August 23, 1975.'

⌘ GREAT WARLEY

It is unusual for a garden to be in the care of the Essex Naturalists' Trust, but Warley Place Gardens had been overgrown and going wild for more than 50 years. John Evelyn, famous for his diary, lived here from 1649 to 1655. He, it is said, introduced the purple crocus to our gardens. It was Miss Ellen Wilmott, living in a much later age, who put the gardens on the map.

Ellen was born in 1858 and moved with her parents and her sister to Warley Place in November 1875. Soon she was involved in planning the gardens, starting with a new alpine garden she designed in 1882, for which she obtained plants from specialists all over the world. She quickly mastered the art of garden design and of propagation. Alongside this interest she developed her hobby of photography and had her own book of photographs published: *Warley Garden in Spring and Summer*.

By 1897 she was elected to the Narcissus Committee of the Royal Horticultural Society. Her parents had died by 1898, her sister had married and moved away. Ellen had inherited no less than £210,000 so she could spend lavishly on her gardens, employing at the height of the splendour of Warley Place, 104 gardeners. Queen Mary and Princess Victoria were frequent visitors, and she dedicated the great published work of her life, *The Genus Rosa* to Queen Alexandra.

From this time though Ellen slid slowly down the slippery slope of over-expenditure. By 1916 she was so much in debt she had to dismiss most of her staff. By 1918 she was taking in lodgers to make ends meet. Yet, even as late as 1932, she sent out a seed list naming over 600 plants. She died on 26th September 1934. The house was sold to a man who did not live there, so the gardens were open to plunder and vandalism. The ruinous old house was demolished in 1939. In 1977 the wilderness that was Warley was leased to the Naturalists' Trust. Volunteers worked at weekends to reduce the jungle to a point where a nature trail could be formed, showing wild and rare, cultivated flora existing side by side.

⌘ GREENSTED-JUXTA-ONGAR

In a Saxon church made of wood, visitors today can claim a unique experience. This is the only such church in our country to have survived into the 21st century. Miller

This Saxon church at Greensted-juxta-Ongar is unique

Christy, writing in 1888, said, 'Although it has been several times restored, it is believed to be the original structure erected as a temporary resting place for the body of St Edmund, on its way from London to Bury St Edmunds in 1013'. He was wrong; with the aid of the latest scientific methods of dating old timber it has been shown that St Andrew's was built nearly 200 years before that, somewhere around the middle of the 8th century.

It is easy to imagine the Saxon settlers here, imbued with all the enthusiasm of their new-found religion, hacking down the trees to make a clearing, then using those very trunks, split down the middle and set up on others laid horizontally, to build the walls of a church. This church has been restored and repaired through 1,100 years, that is something like 55 generations of Greensted people handing on the responsibility from one to another. One generation added the dormer windows in the 16th century and also built the brick chancel. Another, in 1848, replaced the old foundation timbers with a brick plinth.

Greensted Hall, largely Victorian, stands on the same site that was singled out by that Saxon leader as the best place for his abode. These two buildings stand together in the fields, with fine views under glorious skyscapes, still reasonably remote from Chipping Ongar and its development down through Marden Ash. It is a great place to start a walk on the Essex Way which passes by the churchyard gate.

⌘ HADLEIGH

'By far the most important later medieval castle in the county', says Nikolaus Pevsner. But it is now nothing more than a picturesque ruin set against the wide, placid waters of the Thames estuary and the low hills of Kent beyond.

Hubert de Burgh, who had virtually ruled the country during the minority of Henry III, in 1230 obtained royal licence to build this castle. The stone came from Kent and Surrey, brought by barge to the very foot of Castle Hill. Poor Hubert did not enjoy his new castle for it was forfeited to the crown when he was tried on trumped-up charges after falling out of favour.

King Henry and the three succeeding Edwards came to like Hadleigh Castle very much. A governor was appointed to keep the place in readiness for the hunting parties they enjoyed in the extensive forest about it. For ten years from 1360 Edward III set in hand a programme of repair and re-building. It did have some defensive value during the Peasants' Revolt of 1381, when it was manned by the army and sheltered some of the local gentry who feared for their lives. Eventually, it became superfluous to royal requirements and was falling into ruin again when Lord Rich bought it from Edward VI for £700. As Lord Chancellor, he had amassed a fortune and a number of estates in Essex. He had his men cart away loads of the masonry for repair jobs elsewhere. Nature played a part in the despoliation – a landslide carried away all the buildings and the wall on the south side.

The ruined Hadleigh Castle

Its ruins passed on through many hands. Dick Turpin, the early 18th century highwayman, is said to have worked with a gang of smugglers which used the mouldering cellars to hide their contraband. A century later John Constable, the great English painter, captured on canvas the castle in its dying glory. By 1890 it was owned by the Salvation Army when they bought the land to set up a farm colony where men could be given basic training in agriculture to fit them for a new life in the colonies.

⌘ HALSTEAD

In 1825 Samuel Courtauld was to change the town of Halstead when he bought what was then called the Town Mill. Until then it had always ground corn, but Courtauld had a new water wheel put in, not to produce flour, but to drive machinery for weaving material. This innovation led to the mill up river being flooded out by back-up water and he had to introduce a steam-driven beam engine to keep up production. Power looms were added in a separate building in 1832.

By 1843 Courtauld had taken on 1,000 workpeople. His employees were

Townsford Mill, Halstead

appreciative of this benevolent and far-sighted man, at a time when the agricultural depression had caused so much misery and hardship. It was said, 'Both Mr. and Mrs. Courtauld looked personally after the welfare of their workpeople, and were untiring in their efforts for the education, amusement, sustenance, and good housing of every man, woman or child whom they employed'.

Houses with the Courtauld monogram on their gables can still be seen in Bocking and Halstead. Samuel once said, 'When I die, I should like to have written on my tomb, 'He built good cottages'.' – He certainly did! No wonder, then, that 1,600 workpeople got together to present him with a silver medallion at a dinner they arranged in a huge marquee in a field right next to the Courtauld family home at High Garrett in Bocking Street. It was estimated that a four-abreast crocodile of workers a mile long filed into that field to pay honour to their employer.

As part of a great international company Courtauld's work in Halstead has been 'rationalised' and the white, weatherboarded, three storey building we know as Townsford Mill has been given up. It now shelters within its unaltered exterior a series of shops devoted to antiques, arts, crafts, furnishings and so forth.

⌘ HARWICH

This is the port at which, from the earliest times, kings and queens of England have thankfully set foot on Essex soil after rough voyages across the unpredictable North Sea. Their Hanoverian connections from the 18th century onwards meant a great deal of to-ing and fro-ing in and out of Harwich. The High and Low lighthouses were rebuilt in 1818 by the famous engineer John Rennie. At this time they were leased out to a local family, the Rebows, who could charge all shipping using the port a set fee for this important service. When Trinity House took over the lighthouses in 1836, the Rebows were paid £159,730 in compensation, so it shows how profitable this unusual lighthouse business had been.

Yet for all this traffic and the profit it engendered, Harwich nearly dug its own grave. It all started around 1812 when it was found that a kind of cement stone could be quarried from the cliffs to make Roman cement, 'a hydraulic cement made from calcareous nodules from the London Clay', as the dictionary explains. It would set even under water and proved useful so that demand for it soared. A tremendous amount was used in the construction of the great redoubt called Landguard Fort on the other side of the harbour.

The High Lighthouse, Harwich

Everybody wanted this miracle cement, including the builders putting up thousands of Regency houses in London, who found it made an excellent damp-proof stucco. So the local inhabitants went on cutting away the cliffs at Harwich. Once the stone was removed, the soft cliffs were easily eroded by the sea, and a whole headland disappeared. At one time it seemed as if the sea might break through behind the town and cut Harwich off completely. At last the Corporation acted – digging stone at the foot of the cliffs was forbidden and sea defences were put in hand. But what really saved the town from the sea was the invention of Portland cement, which used chalk and was cheaper and stronger.

⌘ HATFIELD PEVEREL

This large village has long been bypassed, but the main street still shows signs of its high road connections with inns, garages and cafes, which constitute a kind of mini-service area. For a more peaceful part press on to the green or to the comparative isolation of the church.

The parish church of St Andrew started out as the nave of the much older chapel of the Benedictine priory, set up as an outlier of St Alban's Abbey. It has been extended and restored through 500 years. When stone could not be obtained, locally-made bricks were used, as can be seen in the stair-turret and battlements of the tower. There is still a Tudor wall around the vicarage garden.

Crix, off the main road towards Boreham, was owned by the Shaen family from 1770 to 1858, giving rise to the Shaen's shaggy dog story. Along the high road, from one of Crix's driveways to the other, a great, fierce, fire-breathing, wild black dog was said to maintain a nightly patrol, offering violence only to those who first attacked it. One waggoner whose horses were frightened by this apparition, struck out at it with his whip. In a flash, man, beasts and wagon were reduced to a pile of hot, smoking ashes. Shaen's Shaggy Dog is not seen these days. Local historian T. M. Hope, writing in 1930, tells us why: 'It is rumoured that he died of spontaneous combustion at his first sight of a motor car'.

⌘ HEMPSTEAD

This is not a village which advertises itself. It hides away seven miles due east of Saffron Walden, yet it could boast of associations with two men of international repute: Dr. William Harvey and Dick Turpin.

Dick Turpin was born in Hempstead, where his parents kept the Bell Inn, now known to the locals as Turpin's Tavern. Dick was apprenticed to a butcher in Whitechapel but soon lost the job because of his wild behaviour. He joined a gang of rustlers and butchered the cattle they stole. He tried smuggling with another gang, then moved on to burglary. By then he had a price of £100 on his head for capture dead or alive. He moved to Epping Forest, where he made a hide-out and started his career as a highwayman on the road which ran through Epping from London to Cambridge.

This was when the hero-worship began, but his glory was short-lived. He shot a man who recognised him and had to move fast to avoid arrest. He went all the way to Yorkshire, poached a pheasant there and, unrecognised, was clapped in jail. His true identity was revealed in a letter to his brother which was intercepted, and the sorry highwayman went to his execution on 7th April 1739.

As a boy he must have played in the churchyard of St Andrew's, which was built in the 15th century. But it is not as he saw it because the tower fell down in 1882, smashing the five bells and seriously damaging the rest of the church. The rebuilding of the tower was not put in hand until 1933; it was interrupted by the last war and was not completed until 1961.

Undisturbed by all the noise the long line of Harveys slept on in the family vault. William Harvey qualified as a doctor when he was 24, in 1602, and went on to discover the circulation of the blood, publishing his findings twelve years later in 1628, *De Motu Cordis*.

His reputation was such that he was appointed royal physician to Charles I. He died on 3rd June 1657, aged 79, and was buried in the family vault. The fall of the tower made the College of Physicians concerned for the continuing safety of the great man's mortal remains. In 1883 his leaden container was moved into a specially built marble sarcophagus in the Harvey Chapel, under a bust by sculptor Edward Marshall.

⌘ HENHAM

'Guests, fish and news grow stale in three days time' says the author of *Strange News out of Essex*, or, *The Winged Serpent*, a pamphlet published in 1669. Even in those days there were people ready to capitalize on the public's gullibility, its fascination with news of a sensational nature. So a printer brought out this news, all about 'The Flying Serpent ... which hath divers times been seen at a parish called Henham-on-the Mount, within 4 miles of Saffron Walden'.

This strange creature had a lair in Birchwood and was first seen on 27th May 1669, when it darted out at a horseman riding by. Then two men saw the serpent as it lay sunning itself on a hillock. They reckoned it was about 9 ft long, tapering from the size of a man's thigh down to the thickness of his leg. It had piercing eyes as big as a sheep's and its teeth looked very white and sharp. They reported, also, that it had two stubby wings protruding from its back, but they appeared altogether too small to enable it to fly.

Many men, brave behind their guns, tried to shoot it, but the serpent was too quick for them. It never did mischief to man or beast, even while it was being hunted down. Then, one day, it was gone, never to return.

There is not much chance of seeing a serpent in Henham today, but it is such a

Henham boasts several thatched cottages

pretty village with its wide-spreading green, thatched-roof cottages and a church which preserves much of its original 13th century fabric that it is certainly worth a visit. In the churchyard, south of the chancel, there is one of those early 19th century graves protected by a stout iron fence anchored to a stone, which were introduced to defeat body-snatchers.

⌘ HIGH EASTER

The first question asked about this place is how on earth it got its name. Easter is a modern rendering of the Old English word for a sheepfold. 'High' denoted the higher situation of the village in comparison with neighbouring Good Easter. Even today it is easy to imagine this gently rolling landscape vibrating with the bleating of thousands of sheep. Their milk and cheese and the cloth from their wool put Essex on the map of medieval Europe.

A nostalgic journey can be made down the narrow lane across from the King William the Fourth at Leaden Roding. It is a scenic journey across the bridge over the diminutive river Can by Lower House Farm and on up the hill past the unusual round house built on the foundations of the old post mill, to the village street and the beautiful old houses dotted about so picturesquely. The church with its lofty tower and prominent stair turret is approached between two timber-framed, gabled houses at least 500 years old.

Round the corner is the village shop. For nearly 50 years Derek Bircher lived there, running the shop, and in the evenings, when the shop was at last closed and the stock replenished and all made tidy for the next day, Derek took up his pen and wrote the history of this village, called, *One Village in History; being an account of the history of High Easter in Essex*. It is a thorough history of the place as well as the story of the life of people through the ages.

New houses have been built where once the blacksmith Christopher Coe helped his father fit the iron rims to cartwheels on the tyring table just outside the forge. He carried on the forge for 43 years until 1949. Then one day he fell ill, left his hammer on the anvil and never went back. His son Eric did not have the heart to move a

High Easter seen from Easterbury Farm

thing, so the forge stood there, exactly as his father had left it, until 1972, when he offered the forge and all its contents to the Chelmsford and Essex Museum. The museum could not afford to dismantle the forge and re-erect it, but every movable object was collected, catalogued and labelled against the day that it could be put on permanent exhibition.

⌘ HIGH RODING

Be warned, the church has to be kept locked due to vandalism. There are directions for obtaining the key. It is a homely enough little village church, with a very attractive Jacobean pulpit rising gracefully like a flower from a central stem. Almost hidden from view, on the floor near the vestry is a brass, nearly 400 years old, with an interesting inscription:

> 'John Jocelyn, esquire, interred here doth lie,
> Sir Thomas Jocelyn's third son of worthy memory.
> Thrice noble was this gentleman by birth, by learning great,

High Roding

By single chast and godly life, he won in heaven a seate;
He the year one thousand and five hundred twentynine was born,
Not twenty yeares old him Cambridge did with two degrees adorn.
King's College him a fellow chose, in anno forty-nine,
In learning tryde whereto he did his mind alwaies incline,
But others took the praise and fame of his deserving wit,
And his inventions as their own, to printing did commit.
One thousand six hundred and three it grieves all to remember,
He left this life (poor's daily friend), the twentyeighth December.'

The church lost its graceful spire when it was burned down by lightning in 1832. High Rodingbury, just below the church, was the old manor house site of Saxon times. Inside its moat a beautiful house still stands there, but it was John Jocelyn's father, Sir Thomas, who moved the centre of administration of the manor when he built New Hall on the bank of the Roding way to the west, in the middle of the 16th century.

⌘ HIGHWOOD

It started out as just a hamlet of Writtle, then it was made a separate ecclesiastical district in 1875 and a civil parish in 1954. Its church had been built as early as 1842 because it was so far for folk to trudge to Writtle, especially in wintry weather. St Paul's is built in warm red brick with a brick-arched bellcote. The bell was originally cast in 1654 by J. Hodson, but after developing a crack, it was melted down and recast in 1921. Inside, the church has been sympathetically modernised, made light and airy, with plain glass windows, except the east window which is a memorial in stained glass to Robert Poole Barlow, who died in 1892.

There are houses in the street which straggles from the church down to Ward's Farm. Past Ward's Farm a left turn down the Ingatestone road leads to early moated sites of habitation like Gorrell's Farm and Awes Farm, reminding us that John Gurel and the Hawys family were living here in the early 14th century. Passing Highwood Cottages and Budd's Farm, where Robert Bode lived in 1327, and climbing up a narrow lane we enter the remains of those woods which gave the settlement its name.

A walk through the wood brings us to the remains of the ancient hermitage, marked on today's maps as Bedeman's Berg. One portion of a wall is all that is left standing of the hermitage. A bush had burst through the foundation of this corner of the wall and had toppled the flint masonry into a great bed of nettles. According to the history book: '... it was a hermitage in the midst of a wood, called Highwood Quarter ... on the abolition of monastic institutions it came to the crown, and was granted to Robert Tyrwhit, Esq, who sold it to Philip Lantall, of whom it was afterwards purchased by Sir William Petre.'

⌘ INGATESTONE

This is a pleasant large village with a hall of Tudor origin, and a church which has a chapel for the resting place of many members of the Petre family, which came up from Devon to build the Hall over ten years from 1539. Old cottages have been demolished so that the handsome brick tower of the church can be appreciated from the main street.

This was a much busier street when it was the main road from London to the east coast. Coaches and travellers brought much trade, so shops and inns grew up to take advantage of it.

Take just one of those inns, the Star. The building was put up in 1480 and 'modernised' in 1643. John Walker's survey for Sir William Petre, Lord of the Manor, made in 1602 includes 'Braynwoods' which was changed into 'Bramwoods' when Anthony Sturgeon, a Chelmsford woollen draper sold it to Jane Aylett. By 1749 it was being leased to Edward White, the local butcher, who set up his slaughterhouse here. By 1850 the premises included a butcher's and a baker's, but when the Chelmsford brewer, Walter Gray bought the building in 1883 it had been a

The gatehouse to Ingatestone Hall

beerhouse for nearly 20 years. The old baker's oven has since been rediscovered and restored as an interesting reminder of the time and trades the Star has seen.

⌘ KIRBY-LE-SOKEN

The name goes back beyond the Conquest. There are three places which stood in what was commonly known as the Liberty of the Sokens: this was one together with Thorpe-le-Soken and Walton-on-the-Naze (then Walton-le-Soken). The Soke, from Anglo-Saxon *Sōch*, signified an area which had been afforded special privileges. One of them may have been connected with the keeping of horses, for Horsey, which means 'Horse-island' is still part of Kirby parish. The extra 'Island' was added to its name as early as the 14th century. That island, with Hedge-end, Skipper and Pewit islands, forms the winding waterways which feed Hamford Water and the Walton Channel north of Kirby.

Down by the quay the outlook in that direction is as wild and wonderful as it was in 1681, the date at which the parish registers began. In those records we can read of a most unusual custom, unique to the Soken villages and observed at least down to 1707. As a token of gratitude for the burial service read over the corpse, the vicar was offered, or even claimed, 'the best upper garment' of the deceased. Surely

Quay Lane, Kirby-le-Soken

the village must have gossiped when they saw their vicar in a coat which so recently belonged to a villager now dead?

The quay is crumbling away these days. It was in a much better state of repair at the end of the 18th century when, before the railway was invented, sea carriage was the easiest way of transporting goods. At this time many a boat came creeping in at night carrying smugglers and the wide variety of goods, from playing cards to coffin nails, which made their nefarious trade so profitable.

⌘ LANGHAM

The Langham Flower Festival in the church of St Mary is an event which adds a

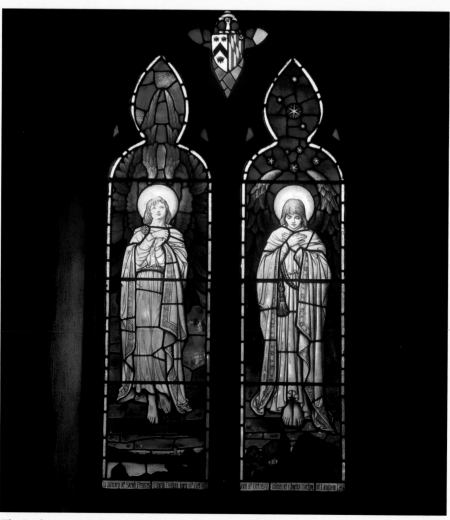

The Darling memorial window in St Mary's church, Langham

real bonus of perfumed pleasure to an expedition into 'Constable Country'. It is, of course, a time when the church can be opened to all comers and there are 'friends' on hand to explain the story. This has been a holy site since Saxon times, though this church was not built until the 12th century. A disastrous fire in 1879, and Victorian 'restoration' before and after it, meant the loss of some of its older fabric and memorials. Through it all the Vigerous family's eternal rest under the centre aisle since 1629 has remained undisturbed. Another local family with an unusual name is the Darlings, living at Langham Hall in the 19th century. Their memorial is the windows of the south aisle. The oldest features in the church today must be the dug-out chest, hollowed out from a trunk of oak. You can see it in a recess of the south wall of the aisle. It is most likely that it was made to receive the money collected for the crusade, in accordance with the decree of 1166.

Walk about the place and be conscious as you do that John Constable enjoyed these woods and fields beside the Stour so much that he made them the subject of several paintings. The main road to the east, the A12, was routed carefully to preserve this area of outstanding beauty. The old main road ran up the steep Gun Hill in the days when the horses hauled such heavy loads that a special notice, cast in iron and painted, was set up at the bottom:

> THE DUMB ANIMALS HUMBLE PETITION
> Rest, Drivers, rest on this steep hill,
> Dumb Beasts pray use with all good will.
> Goad not, scourge not, with thonged whips,
> Let not one curse escape your lips.
> God sees and hears.

⌘ LEIGH-ON-SEA

It is hard to divine in the maze of roads and railway, bridges and Broadway, sports and shopping centres, the old Leigh which H. Lewis Jones looked at in 1892, when he spoke of a foreground of fishing bawleys, a line of straggling cottages along Leigh creek, backed by others rising in tiers irregularly above each other to the grand old church at the top of the hill.

In those days nearly all the inhabitants were connected with shrimping, from making the boats, sailing them, dredging up the shrimps, boiling them, packing them and selling them. The boats, called bawleys, were specially built to draw no more than 6 ft of water, though they weighed 20 tons and carried a big spread of sail. They all went off in the morning mist like great ghostly birds, ready to shoot their trawls as soon as they reached the shrimping grounds. In the evening they would come back up the estuary on the flood tide.

The shrimpers carried big coppers on board and boiled the shrimps on the way back to port. At the quayside in those days Lewis Jones remembered buying a delicious tea – shrimps and watercress, bread and butter, and a pot of tea – all for ninepence a head; less than fourpence today! Down by the Peter Boat pub, so called because St Peter is the patron saint of fishermen, you can still see the boats come in and buy yourself a tasty tub of shellfish – but don't think of comparing prices!

There is no trace of the old shipyard where the king's ships were built, but the dedicated pedestrian can find interesting walks where old inns and unusual houses are reminders of that time, and later days when Leigh's smugglers challenged the revenue men in their own miniature sea battles.

⌘ LITTLE BADDOW

The church's situation halfway down the hill, just off the lane and under a spreading tree, is most inviting. Six hundred years ago a man and a woman, important in the community, were interred here. Their tomb chests stand there still, and on them, carved life-size in wood, lie their effigies.

Some 500 years ago an artist stood on primitive scaffolding within the church and painted the walls in glowing colours with pictures and texts from the holy scriptures. Time passed, beliefs changed. All that is left of the artist's pious work in the name of his Lord is part of a painting of St Christopher bearing the infant Jesus across the water. It had been covered up for centuries with layers of plaster and lime, which were scraped away so patiently in 1920.

On up the road is the General's Arms with its big bay windows either side of the front door and a sign which evokes the memory of Major General William Goodday Strutt, brother of the first Lord Rayleigh. Born in 1762, he became an ensign in the 51st Regiment when he was just 16. He was a brigadier by the time he was 33 and was still on very active service on 8th January 1796, when he was severely injured by a musket ball. That ball is still on view in the other family home, Terling Place, labelled, 'The Ball that Shattered my Leg'.

For walkers the places in this parish must either be the banks of the Chelmer below the church or the 80 acres of Blakes Wood above it.

⌘ LITTLE DUNMOW

The church here is such a strange-looking building. The body is like a barn with buttresses and windows of beautiful tracery. Beside it stands the campanile, what Nikolaus Pevsner, the architectural expert calls, 'a silly turret'. It was built of brick by James Brown, a Braintree builder, in 1872. I find it heartening to think that a church founded in 1104 as part of the priory should still be under repair and further embellishment nearly 900 years later. It has to be kept locked these days, but it really is an experience to get the key and stand alone in this simple church of St Mary the Virgin.

The famous flitch chair in the church at Little Dunmow

Because the villagers were allowed to use the Augustinian priory chapel from time immemorial, that part of the priory was preserved to them at the Dissolution of the Monasteries.

One of the most touching sights in the church today is the memorial to villagers who fell in the First World War. Beautiful decoration was carried out in plaster, which through the years has crumbled so much that half the design is missing, but you will see fresh flowers placed upon it. Look at the chair in the chancel. Obviously knocked up from secondhand ecclesiastical timber dated to the 13th century, it is said to be one of the original chairs in which winners of the famous Dunmow Flitch ceremony were carried shoulder-high round the village. The flitch was originally given by the priory here; only in modern times did the enactment of the ceremony move over to Great Dunmow.

⌘ LITTLE EASTON

This is such a peaceful place and, with the river close by and a lot of good hedgerows, it is a pleasant place in which to walk about. You may, like us, get a chance to add to your own garden from the plants on sale at garden gates as you stroll down Duck Street.

The visitor can find refreshment at the Stag, before walking via Manor Road down the path to the church, St Mary's. This is the place to see monuments, particularly to the Maynard family, from 1610, down to the graceful bust of Frances.

Her father died when she was three years old, in 1864, and, very unusually, she was made heir to his estate. In a glittering life, which she describes in her autobiography, *Life's Ebb and Flow*, published in 1929, she was inspected by Queen Victoria as a possible wife for her youngest son, actually married Lord Brooke who inherited the Earldom of Warwick, became mistress of the Prince of Wales, and then took up the socialist cause.

She still entertained on the grand scale at Easton Lodge while slipping into grave debt. In desperation she arranged to publish the Prince's love letters to her;

Easton Lodge, Little Easton

then, saying she had received an offer of £100,000 from a publisher, she asked for that sum from King George V, upon receipt of which she would give him all the letters. The Royal lawyers obtained a court order; the letters were destroyed in their envelopes forthwith. 'Darling Daisy', as the Prince had called her, had her debts paid and no more was said. She lived on in her tottering mansion until 1938, when she died, aged 77. The old house was burned down around 1946 and subsequently demolished.

⌘ LOUGHTON

Midway in Loughton's High Road, stands Lopping Hall. To explain its name and the reason for its being built in 1884 we must tell a story.

In the second half of the 19th century great tracts of the old forest of Epping were literally being stolen by local landowners who extended their boundaries, then sold off the land to developers. In 1865 the Lord of the Manor of Loughton enclosed 1,316 acres of the forest, put a high fence all round it and started the wholesale felling of the trees to make roads to serve new houses. Just one man stood in his way. He was Thomas Willingale, who insisted that he had the ancient right to go into the forest in winter months and lop off the lower branches of trees for fuel.

His sons and his neighbours supported him. They climbed the fence and lopped the trees, and got seven days hard labour for their pains. But Thomas persisted and won sympathy and support from people of influence, who helped him take his case to the Master of the Rolls. The poor old chap died before the case was settled, but it was his doggedness which caught the imagination of the nation, stopped the further development and decimation of the forest and ended up with Queen Victoria travelling to Epping forest on 6th May 1882 to declare it an open public space forever. The City of London stepped in with the cash to buy out all the other interests, paying £250,000. It not only compensated the lords it also remembered the loppers, and the money paid for the extinction of their acknowledged rights was used to build Lopping Hall.

⌘ MALDON

Maldon is a must for people who like to potter about where there are small boats and peaceful waters. Its history is there to be seen. First look on the OS map south east of the town and you will see the crossed swords symbol denoting the site of the battle of Maldon in AD 991.

The Vikings had come up the river Blackwater on a raiding expedition and had camped on Northey Island. In trying to stop them the Saxons made a terrible mistake; they let the Vikings cross the causeway from the island at low tide and form up on the mainland, when they should have picked them off one at a time on

Maldon's waterfront

the narrow crossing. The Saxons lost the battle – and most of their finest warriors.

In the town there are three churches that prove the age and importance of this old port. One of them, St Peter's, was ruinous as early as 1665. Against its 15th century tower Dr Thomas Plume, born here in 1630, had a school built from the ruins of the nave, and over it a library, to which he left all his books and pictures, with a bequest to ensure their upkeep. Climb up the winding stone stairway, enter the door and you step into the 17th century. All the books are bound in leather, placed on wooden presses or in great wooden chests in a place of great peace and atmosphere of scholarship.

Whilst in the burial register of the church of All Saints, you can read the oft-repeated tale of Edward Bright who weighed more than 42 stone. He died at the age of 29 and needed a coffin 6ft 7ins long, 3ft 6ins wide and 3ft deep.

From the bridge at the bottom of Market Hill there is a pleasant walk with riverside views down to the quay beside the Queen's Head, where there are several barges moored. Their great masts, red sails and complicated rigging are a challenge to photographers. The Queen's Head is an intriguing public house, dating back beyond the existing deeds, which date from 1700. Its bars are crammed with photographs, paintings and drawings of anything and everything to do with ships. It is like a museum in itself, but the official museums are the Maritime Museum nearby and the Maldon Museum in the High Street.

⌘ MANNINGTREE

Essex is renowned for its witches and for the trials, hangings and burnings of poor, ignorant and innocent old women, and one or two men, in the 16th and 17th centuries. There had been witch trials at the assizes in Chelmsford as early as 1566, but the revival, in the 1640s, of the witch scare was largely due to one man, a lawyer who lived here in Manningtree, named Matthew Hopkins. He noted the growing superstition of these troubled times and saw the deep fear local people had of witchcraft. He himself may have believed that so-called witches could make their neighbours sicken and die or spread disease amongst cattle and sheep or simply spoil the butter in the churn. He certainly saw a good way to make a nice, fat profit out of it.

In 1644 he said he had approached Parliament and obtained a commission from them to go on a witch-hunting tour of the eastern counties. He was to be paid a set sum for each witch he found. Thus armed, he found a lot of witches, torturing people to extract confessions, and thereby his fee. He also extracted money from the parish authorities as a kind of tip for ridding them of witches – just like a ratcatcher!

By 1645 he had arrested 200 people and clapped them in gaol. Sixty-eight of them were hanged or burned at the stake. He even wrote a pamphlet setting out all the points in favour of his evil work. No wonder he was called 'The Witchfinder General'. Some people say that when the witchcraft scare had passed and he was denounced he retired discreetly to Mainningtree, to die in his bed; others say that he was challenged, and hanged. Nobody knows.

⌘ MARGARETTING

One very attractive feature in the centre of Margaretting is the village sign, a representation of St Margaret and the church, carved in wood by Harry Carter of Swaffham. It was bought with funds accruing from the Queen's Silver Jubilee celebrations and put up in April 1978 on the very brink of the village pond. That pond had been in danger of loss through neglect until Essex Conservation Volunteers cleaned it out and created the haven for water fowl it is now.

The reredos in St Margaret's church, Margaretting

Walk the footpaths down to the church across the railway and see the reredos, carved not by famous artists, but by the local men attending the wood-carving classes instructed by Charles Jennings at the building yard in Penny Lane early in the 20th century. St Margaret's is essentially of 15th century construction with an amazing timber tower, belfry and spire. Most of the church is contemporary with it, including the north porch, also carried out in timber.

The east window shows a feature now of great rarity. In stained glass, much restored, but still impressive in its three-light 15th century composition, a 'Tree of Jesse' is depicted, showing how Christ was descended from Jesse, the father of David.

⌘ MATCHING

To the best of my knowledge there is only one Wedding Feast House in Essex. Yet what a generous and understanding thought lies at the bottom of it. Back in the days when dates hardly mattered and a marriage was a solemn affair celebrated in the presence of God in the parish church, half the village would be related to the bride and the groom and they all wanted to join in the celebration of such a joyous occasion. Finding a room large enough was a problem, and an expense.

A man called Chimney had a row of cottages built, of which the upper storey was separate, with its own staircase. This was the room that he provided for those wedding feasts. Although the guide book of a 100 years ago reports it as 'ruinous', it has been most sympathetically restored and can be seen keeping the church of St Mary company amidst oak and chestnut trees.

Add to this the Hall on the other side of the lane, the water-filled moat which laps it round and the fine, big dovecote which once supplied the lord with his winter meat and you have what some writers might call a 'time capsule'.

The Wedding Feast House sits next to the church at Matching

⌘ MERSEA ISLAND

Comes a fine day and families in Essex seem to say, 'Let's go to Mersea' – and a tailback of cars soon queues to cross the Strood, the only access to the island. The Strood has connected it directly to the mainland since it was first built by the Romans as a causeway. 'Strood' (Old English *Strōd*) meant marshy ground; it originally applied to the muddy channel but somehow the name was transferred to the roadway itself.

The Romans left behind a wheel tomb, a type reasonably common in the other parts of their empire but rare in this country. Its site, a private garden some 200 yards east of the church of West Mersea, was discovered and excavated in 1896. It is a big affair – a circular wall 65ft in diameter and 3ft thick, with internal walls radiating like spokes from a small central chamber.

Barrow Hill, on the north side of the island's central plateau, was excavated in 1912 and found to be about 23 ft high and 110 ft round. It was a big mound to dig through, and all that was found, right at the centre was a tiny chamber 18 inches square and just a little more than that high. In that small space was a casket made of lead, and within that was a glass vessel containing the remains of the cremation of a human body. What an important person he or she must have been!

But forget the past and enjoy the present on the beach at West Mersea, or drive to the eastern end, now protected as a country park.

⌘ MISTLEY

When building council houses at New Mistley in 1946, workmen found a burial urn with incinerated remains – not the only evidence of Roman life here. From very early times the place grew and prospered with its wharves on the river Stour. It owed its continuing success to Richard Rigby whose father Edward had bought the Hall in 1680. Richard inherited it, rebuilt it in a 700 acre park and had it judged by Horace Walpole as 'The charmingest place by Nature, and the most trumpery by art ...' It was demolished in 1845. As Coller, writing in 1861 says, 'The land thus set free gave greater scope to industry – allowed commerce more elbow-room for its efforts ...'

Richard had intended that the New Mistley which he planned and built down to the river should be more than a commercial centre with granaries, malting and warehouses; it should be a spa, and to this end decorative features were included in the development of the place. One of them, a little square with a fountain graced by a swan can still be seen.

The rebuilding of the church in 1735 was part of Rigby's plan, but his son, also Richard, had it completely redesigned again in 1776 by the great Robert Adam, with an elegant tower at each end of the nave. That nave was pulled down when yet another church was built but the towers remain as 'classified' monuments to

Mistley's swan fountain

Mistley's magnificent past. One of the great sights today is the flock of swans, which glide along the river.

⌘ MOUNTNESSING

Mountnessing windmill was reopened in 1983. It had been put in full working order under the supervision of one of the last millwrights to practise the craft, Vincent Pargeter. Essex County Council has owned the mill since 1956, when it stood as an interesting but dilapidated and deteriorating landmark just off the old A12.

The Prince of Wales public house was, in fact, a bakery in earlier days, getting its flour straight from the mill across the road, which had been standing since 1807 at least. That was the date offered by Robert Agnis, whose family ran the mill throughout its working life down to 1924, and then again for a short period in 1932–3. This was not the first mill on this site. There is evidence of a windmill on the mound as early as 1477, and Ogilby and Morgan's map of 1678 shows a mill still working there.

In the 19th century the 'round house' – the brick built base through which the strong central post rose up to take the whole weight of the mill – was thatched. It made a charming picture; the white clapboard mill and sails rising above the golden thatch and the warm red brick of the perfectly circular base. Rats ruined the thatch, its replacement was uneconomic so, in 1919, it was replaced with tarred boards.

In the 1930s the poor old mill went into a decline, aggravated in May 1949 when it was struck by lightning, but then, when all seemed lost, the County Council took it over and it was restored to working order. Full details of this attractive old mill, historical and technical, can be found in the late K. G. Farries' *Essex Windmills, Millers and Millwrights*.

⌘ NEWPORT

'Port' in earlier days denoted a town, usually one with a charter for a market. So this village became a town when the market was transferred from Clavering or some neighbouring place in the 12th century. But it did not keep that status for long, for Saffron Walden had the market transferred to it in the same century. Many of the old houses are still standing. Even the old prison, a good-looking building of the 18th century, has been converted to superior dwellings.

There was a time in the 16th century when the Guildhall, or Town House, presented to the inhabitants by Robert Driver in 1544, stood empty with the diminution of trade. This is where Mrs Joyce Frankland comes into the picture. Having been widowed twice, her life centred round her only son. He was riding to London in 1581 when his horse threw him and he was killed. Her grief knew no bounds. One friend who came expressly to console her was the Dean of St Paul's. He said, 'Comfort yourself, good Mistress Frankland and I will tell you how you shall have twenty good sonnes to comfort you in these your sorrows which you take for this one sonne.'

So he sowed the germ of an idea. It grew and bore fruit in 1588, when with further encouragement from friends, Joyce started a school in the former Guildhall and engaged a master at £20 per annum. In 1837 that building was demolished so that a new school might be built there with room for 60 boys on the first floor. The ground floor was rented out – as a granary! When Saffron Walden's grammar school was closed, children from that area were found places here at Newport – a kind of quid pro quo for losing their market to Saffron Walden all those years ago.

⌘ PANFIELD

The heart of this little settlement, 'open country on the banks of the Pant', as the Saxons described it, is its parish church which stands a little to the east of the later development of the village. It is mostly a 15th century rebuilding, with walls of flint and pebble rubble, but it has had to be restored through that time, as is evident from the timber-framing of its south porch.

There is a nice story here about the way in which one old inhabitant is remembered. Edward Bangs, baptised at the font here on 28th October 1591 took the dangerous passage to the new American colony and religious freedom. He prospered and his descendant, Mr W. E. Nickerson of Boston, Massachusetts came to his ancestor's village and gave ornaments and utensils for worship in his memory. Another memorial is the church clock: it celebrates Queen Victoria's Golden Jubilee in 1897.

Panfield Hall lies to the south of the church. Its oldest part, on the west side, dates from 1546. The eastern part was completed in 1583. It looks a handsome place in a peaceful landscape.

One man who lived in the rectory here for 26 years in the latter half of the 17th century was John Ouseley. He was a pioneer in the collection of historical information about Essex. His collected papers, which never reached print themselves, were a terrific help to later historians, like the great Philip Morant, and they were not slow to acknowledge their debt. Yet the Reverend John Ouseley was such a humble and unassuming man that nothing is now known of his own personal history.

⌘ PLESHEY

Pleshey owes its name to the Normans. At one time it was called Tumblestown because of all the old entrenchments, mounds, ditches and tumuli which each wave of settlers had raised or dug to defend themselves or bury their dead. The Normans called it Pleshey because, in their old French language that meant an enclosure made by growing a thick hedge, preferably a prickly blackthorn, and bending it back on itself by interlacing the branches.

This is a place which, since its mention in Shakespeare, has been fully covered in the history books and the tourist literature, but one thing has been left out. Pleshey is the home of the Darby Steam Digger. Thomas Churchman Darby, a farmer here, was of a mechanical turn of mind. In 1877 he planned a steam-driven machine which would turn the rotary motion of the engine into a heavy digging action.

The prototype of his machine was, in fact, too ingenious. It actually 'walked' along, digging as it went, but when its cast-iron components came up against stones in the soil they shattered like glass. Darby persevered, he had his digger made in steel and showed it at the Royal Agricultural Show in 1880, where it won a prize. But farmers were so very conservative, they could not envisage ploughing without the plodding horse, and so the digger was not a commercial success, though around Pleshey, where people saw it in action, you could see seven of them at work.

Now everything on the farm is mechanised, automated, computerised, but the Darby Digger has gone. There is not one working part left in the world to be a monument to that remarkable man, so much in advance of his time.

⌘ PURLEIGH

All Saints' church, Purleigh

What place in Essex can connect England with America and Russia in one short span of years? It is Purleigh, ten miles south east of Chelmsford.

The Americans paid for the restoration of the 13th century tower of All Saints' church in 1892 because Lawrence Washington, who had been rector here from 1632 to 1643, was great-grandfather of their first President.

The Russians invaded in 1897. A group of them, including some English sympathisers, came from Croydon to found a colony of brotherhood here, living simple lives of self-sufficiency on 16 acres either side of the lane from Cock Clarks to Cold Norton. They trod their own clay, made their own bricks and built their own houses. The first of them is now known as Grey House and another is called Colony House. They tilled their fields, gathered their crops, and all seemed sweetness and light for the 80-odd anarchists. But within a couple of years they had fallen out among themselves, disbanded their brotherhood and gone their separate ways. Only those strongly built houses stand as their memorial.

⌘ RAYNE

The focal point of Rayne today is the church. Before it was rebuilt, in 1840, it gave rise to a saying: 'It won't be long before you're saying your prayers at Rayne'. This goes way back to the 14th century, when the wife of the Lord of the Manor, John de Naylinhurst, was having a terrible labour. Some of her attendants went to the church, to the altar erected to the worship of the Virgin Mary in the south aisle, and prayed for their lady. They were astonished when they saw the statue of the

Virgin smile in answer to their prayers and flew back to the house to be met with the good news that her ladyship was safely delivered. For many years after that, expectant women made their way to the church to pray for a successful pregnancy and a prompt delivery.

After being closed for six years from 1834 the church was rebuilt, but the strong Tudor brick tower was retained and restored. It gives the church such a sturdy, solid personality. In a glass case under the tower can be seen a knight's helm. It is only a replica. The story is told in *A View into Essex*: 'Sir Giles Capell, Lord of the Manor, was one of the Knights led by Henry VIII who challenged all comers from the continent for thirty days at the Field of the Cloth of Gold in 1520. In his will he wrote: 'I will that my beste helmett and my armying Sworde be sett over my funeralls according to the devise of the harrauld.' They remained in position over his tomb in the church until the 1840 restoration, when the Capell tombs were unaccountably destroyed and the armour removed by the builder. The helm was sold to a Miss Courtauld who gave it to a friend who sold it for a great sum to an American. It is now in the Metropolitan Museum of Art, New York.

⌘ RETTENDON

The parish of Rettendon is strangely shaped like the head of an alsatian with its nose pointing to Hanningfield reservoir. A journey round it offers many points of interest. The Bell inn has quietly gone on giving rest and refreshment to travellers for 200 years. The village has been much extended as we can see from the fact that Curds Farm, now in amongst houses and bungalows, has actually been given a street number. Past Buckhatch Farm there is a private road to Hyde Hall, on the site of a house which was here as early as 1412, when it was called Le Hide. In 1993 Hyde Hall Gardens, comprising 24 acres, were donated to the Royal Horticultural Society.

'Mill House' on a gate – and a green mound behind the house are the last reminders of Rettendon windmill. There was a mill here before 1678; then a new one was built in 1797 – and its sails swept so low that three-year-old Elizabeth Jefferies, wandering near them, was struck and fatally wounded. In 1853 the miller's 24-year-old son, George Borrodell, risked pushing a wheelbarrow past the mill as the sails were turning; he was caught by the downward swish of a sail, and lived but five hours. Finally, on 3rd January 1873 the ill-fated mill caught fire and was burned down, despite the valiant efforts of the horsedrawn fire engine summoned from Chelmsford.

Rettendon Hall recalls memories of the Humfreys, who lived here from 1605 to 1727. The line ended with bachelor Edmund Humfrey. He it was who arranged for his own splendid monument which spans the breadth of the north aisle of the church. He reclines, in effigy, on a pedestal, pointing heavenwards with his left hand.

⌘ RIVENHALL

According to archaeologists, 'In a rural situation an example of the continued occupation of a villa after the historical end of Roman Britain is provided by Rivenhall. There it can be seen how two large domestic buildings and an aisled barn were modified during the 4th, 5th, and 6th centuries to suit the needs of the agriculturally based estate.' When the church of St Mary and All Saints was restored a Saxon window was reopened, and all around the church evidence has been found of continuous human occupation of this site from Roman times.

Probably the best known person to be born in this small village is Thomas Tusser, who saw the light of day here in 1523. He was what might be termed the Farmers' Poet, with his *The Hundreth Good Pointes of Husbandrie*, published in 1557 and revised in 1573 to no less than 500 'good points'. He was not much good at farming himself and tried various moves about the country. On his death it was said, 'He spread his bread with all sorts of butter, but none would stick thereon'.

Nevertheless, his poetry lives on; advice on farming and housekeeping written in rhyming couplets. He goes all through the year with the jobs to be done but at Christmas he relaxes a bit:

'Good husband and housewife, now chiefly be glad
Things handsome to have, as they ought to be had.
They both do provide, against Christmas to come,
To welcome their neighbours, good cheer to have some.
Good bread and good drinke, a good fire in the hall,
Brawn, pudding, and souse, and good mustard withal.
Beef, mutton and pork, and good pies of the best,
Pig, veal goose and capon, and turkey well dressed,
Cheese, apples and nuts, and good carols to hear,
As then, in the country is counted good cheer.'

⌘ ROCHFORD

You always know where you are in Rochford – with North Street, East Street, South Street and West Street, and the Market Square in the middle, it is as good as a compass to the traveller. The parish church of St Andrew shows its age in 15th century architecture and the rebuilding of its tower in warm, red brick a century later.

A church of another kind is remembered in Chapel Cottages in North Street. It was once the chapel of the Peculiar People, a religion now merged with the Union of Evangelical Churches. It all started when James Banyard, a shoemaker in this town, went to hear a couple of evangelists putting forth their message with missionary zeal. That message caught his imagination. He was inspired to preach

South Street, Rochford

himself and so impressed a meeting that they continued as his own congregation and, in 1838, built their own chapel. Their name was taken from the Bible. The general message of simple faith spread through the villages both sides of the Crouch and more chapels were built, even though the congregations were of the poorest people.

A hundred years ago it would have been a regular Sunday sight as these country people, so happy in their faith, walked along to chapel together, carrying the dishes and bowls which contained their dinners. These were put on the big central stove which heated the chapel to warm up nicely while their owners spent the day in prayer and praise and preaching. With a break for dinner, of course.

⌘ ROXWELL

Roxwell is just a sleepy village, on the road to nowhere, so there are a good many Roxwell folk, born and bred in the village, to hand down lore and legend to the new generation. One of their stories is about the day the boiler burst.

It happened at the watermill just off the end of the village street. The wheel was turned by the rather uncertain flow of the Roxwell brook until a steam engine was installed. From 1868, when that engine was already working, right down to 1926, the mill ground its flour under the watchful eye of John Shepherd Ray and his son Ernest. Nobody knew when the steam engine was actually installed with its massive boiler over 12 ft height and $4^1/_2$ ft in diameter.

Ernest carried on with it after his father's death in 1889 and had it checked and overhauled in 1899. On 5th February 1901, very early in the morning, Ernest lit the fire beneath the boiler. By 7.15 am it had reached its operating pressure. The safety valve did not blow off to give any warning. Suddenly, with a very loud bang, the boiler exploded, and took off like a rocket. It soared into the air, striking a corner of the mill roof on the way, and landed some 60 ft away, only yards from the houses, and the people, on the village street. What a commotion! But Ernest had it all repaired and it carried on for another 25 years.

In 1950 the mill was converted to an unusual and interesting house by sandwiching the clapboard and timber-beamed construction between two thick layers of concrete. That is why doors and windows appear so irregularly – they are the original openings put in to suit the convenience of the mill.

⌘ SAFFRON WALDEN

If you want to be lost for a moment in olden times take a look at the house in Church Street which was once the Sun Inn, where Cromwell ordered his men to seek the King and bring him in for trial. You will see that the plaster on its gable has been worked into a wonderful picture, in deep relief, of two men having a fight. One has a mighty club, formed from the axletree of a cart, with a wheel from that same cart as a shield, while the other fellow seems to be equipped only with the normal sword and buckler.

The story goes that Tom Hickathrift owned a meadow in which 30,000 sheep were grazed. The villagers disputed his right to the land. When he would not give in they decided to turn up in a bunch and threaten him. Tom picked up his axletree and defeated them. The story grew with the telling, and the pargeter, or plasterer, thought it would make a very nice subject for the Sun Inn when it was redecorated in 1676.

Everybody knows that this town was famous for the saffron crocus grown in medieval times for its gorgeous yellow dye as much as for its use in cooking. But 100 years ago it was just as famous for its hollyhocks. After a day bent over his last, Charlie Baron, a shoemaker in the town, was glad to get out in his garden, where his hobby was hollyhocks. He crossed them and recrossed them until he had a bower of flowers in wonderful new shades, and semi-doubles too. He did it just for love of the plant. It was very fortunate that William Chater, a professional nurseryman, knew Charlie and could take over his experiments.

In 1847 he issued what was then the most comprehensive catalogue of named varieties of hollyhock, and he revised it every year to 1873 with a continuing variety of new types and colours. Then disaster struck. A terrible infection spread throughout his nurseries and all those beautiful varieties sickened and died. For years not a hollyhock was to be had while new techniques of raising disease-free plants were evolved.

But William Chater did triumph over his tribulation, and before he died in 1885 he passed on his knowledge to Webb and Brand who could claim, in 1900, to be the largest growers of hollyhocks in the world.

⌘ ST OSYTH

Thousands of people enjoy holidays in chalets and caravans along its five-mile coastline. Actually this place was first called Chich, from the Saxon word for a bend, because the first settlement here was by a bend in the creek which runs down to Colne estuary. In later days the name became Chich St Osyth, and now the 'Chich' is quite forgotten. So how did St Osyth creep in? This is the story.

Osyth was the daughter of the great Frithewald, King of the East Saxons, She grew up in the Christian faith and became prioress of a nunnery founded here by her father in the tiny settlement of Chich. In the autumn of AD 653 a band of Danish raiders came up the creek in their boats, pulled them ashore here and went on the rampage. They broke into Osyth's nunnery intent on humiliating the nuns

The splendid gate house at St Osyth's Priory

and subjecting them to sexual harassment, as it might be called today. Osyth stood before them and faced up to the Danish chief. He demanded that the nuns deny their faith; she rejected his demand. He, in his wrath, ordered her to be beheaded, and one of his men immediately carried out the dreadful deed.

Osyth died for her faith and for her nuns. Legend has it that she straightaway bent down, picked up her head and carried it to the church where she struck the door with her bloodstained hand to indicate that she should be buried there. On the spot where she was beheaded a spring of the purest water flowed forth from that very moment – and the place is still known as Nun's Wood today. She was canonised, and we only think of St Osyth as a nice place for a holiday.

⌘ SALCOTT

The name of this parish, meaning salt house, is one of the clues in trying to identify the mysterious red hills, which extend down the coast from Clacton to Goldhanger.

Church ruins at Salcott-cum-Virley

The hills are, in fact, man-made mounds, about 2,500 years old. Some of them are up to 30 acres in extent, even though they rise no more than 5 ft above the original soil.

The soil has not been dug out and heaped: this is the accumulation of waste product left behind by man. There are hundreds of these red hills, despite the fact that many of them have been ploughed away or overtaken by the sea. The history books are very cagey about what they were, but, putting two and two together, adding clues like the name of this village and other places in the area, the answer could be – salt. Ancient man needed salt. He collected it from the seashore, dried out from tide-forsaken pools by the summer sun. He divined that sea water could be boiled away to leave its salty deposit. That salt could be traded far inland for other vital necessities like tools, weapons and hides. So the Salcott man made big, wide, shallow pans of thick, crude pottery, put them as near the tide as he could, filled them with sea water, then lit a fire beneath them using the brushwood and timber he could gather on the foreshore. All he had to do when the water was boiled away was to scrape up the salt.

Sometimes the pans broke and their pieces were simply left lying in the growing pile of ashes. Imagine the amount of ashes and other detritus which would accumulate over centuries of salt making in this manner. Roman pottery found in these red hills shows that the salt industry in this area was carried on down to Christian times.

⌘ SOUTHMINSTER

This is a strange place of old and new. Estates have sprouted off a main street, which is itself having to alter to cater for the growing population. It is a bustling place, but there is a phrase in the Essex guide of 1887 – 'It has a Reading Room, a Coffee Tavern, and Gas Works' which shows Southminster was already an urban if not to say urbane place of residence over a 100 years ago. Today the railway takes people to their London connections and commuters are prepared to arrive home late for the pleasures of living way out in the Essex countryside, halfway between the estuaries of the Blackwater and the Crouch. Due east there is just one lane which peters out in the Dengie marshes, still a wonderfully wild place where tracks and paths lead on to the sea wall and splendid views out across the North Sea.

Opposite the Memorial Hall the church of St Leonard has the most untidy-looking architecture of any church in the county. Even Nikolaus Pevsner calls it odd and aesthetically unsatisfactory. But forget the building, some of the furniture in the vestry is very interesting – a chart table, a bureau, a mirror, even the fireplace, were all once the personal property of Admiral Lord Nelson. They are here because Dr Alexander Scott, who was appointed vicar of Southminster in 1806 had sailed away with Nelson on his conquering campaigns as his chaplain and secretary. He it was who comforted the great man in his dying on the *Victory*, and when the ship came back to port he took these items with him as personal, sad reminders.

⌘ STANFORD RIVERS

There are not many places which have the Lord of the Manor ready to research and write their history. Harold M. Scott did just this for Stanford Rivers in 1974. He gives such snippets of information as would slip through the net of a dry historian. For example, in October 1817 the villagers were so plagued by sparrows that the churchwardens offered 4d for every dozen dead sparrows brought to them and 2d a dozen for their eggs. As to the look of the place he says: 'Here we find a very scattered population, divided into two distinct areas ... the passing motorist sees little of interest and is naturally quite unaware of the many interesting features revealed by my story of its past.'

St Margaret's church is described in detail from its founding around 1150 to the additions of the bell turret and spire in the 15th century and the west porch in 1812. In 1944 the whole south side of the church felt the blast of a German flying bomb. It was all carefully repaired; then in 1974 workmen on the bell tower and spire had some sort of accident and the whole thing was gutted by fire and once again restoration was required.

The Congregational chapel, started in a cottage on the main road at Little End, moved to a purpose built chapel in 1820 and saw David Livingstone, then a student missionary at Chipping Ongar, step up to the pulpit to preach the sermon. He gave out the text, was totally overcome by stage fright, blurted out, 'Friends, I have forgotten all I had to say', and stepped down again.

On the main road stands the former Ongar Union Workhouse, now a flag and tent factory, established by Messrs Piggott in 1927.

⌘ STANSTED MOUNTFITCHET

What a grand name for such a small place – too much for modern advertising executives – the airport which has made this place famous round the world is simply called Stansted. Though that airport has bought up acres more land and demolished old houses or had them rebuilt elsewhere, it does not impinge to any great extent on the life of the small town two miles to the west on the other side of the M11. The nearest building to that road is the parish church of St Mary, with its impressive brick tower built in 1662. In the north chapel there is a tomb chest with an effigy of a knight in armour. It was probably carved in the late 12th or early 13th century and may well be the resting place of Richard Mountfitchet, of the family which was rewarded by the Conqueror with 48 Essex manors.

They made their headquarters here and built a castle northwest of the church. Soon after Richard died, the line failed and the castle began to crumble; only its

The reconstructed Norman village at Stansted Mountfichet

keep was made of stone. There was practically nothing left of it until a new man bought the land, saw the potential public interest in such an old site and set about restoring it. The Norman motte and bailey castle has been 'replicated' and the village reconstructed. As the guide says, visitors can see a 'Complete living village and Castle'. There is no doubt that it all adds up to a great day out in the summer.

Then there is the windmill in the west of the town which advertises itself with its strong, tall brick tower. It is open on certain days through the summer, giving visitors a chance to see the internal workings of a mill built in 1787 which worked until 1910 and was put back into working condition by the second Lord Blyth and presented to the town in 1934.

⌘ STEBBING

A church all built of stone in our stoneless county is a rare sight. Small wonder then that visitors head for St Mary's. It looks the perfect parish church with its spire above its buttressed tower and two rows of windows which flood the place with light. The building is all of a piece, put up in the 14th century. The feature really to be enjoyed within is the very unusual stone rood screen stretching across the chancel arch with its delicately carved patterns. There is only one other stone rood screen like it in the whole county, and that is at Great Bardfield.

There is another place which any visitor should go to see, down on the Stebbing brook. As Hervey Benham says in *Some Essex Watermills*, 'Here, away on its own, down the lane beside the White Hart Inn, is a fine example of an 18th century corn mill, standing on one of Stebbing's two Domesday sites'. The beautiful white-painted clapboard mill, under its tiled roof and jutting lucam, contrasts with the green of the trees which have grown up about it, beside the brook.

It was being worked by miller Robert Dixon in 1823, Joseph Dixon followed him for 20 years; then the Choppings took it on until 1882. From that year Henry Ruffel took over and employed a young man who had already started there in 1863. His sons followed him and were able to buy the mill in 1931. Len Hynds, grandson of that young man, went into the mill as a school leaver in 1945 and became the owner and miller in 1959. Ken Ellis, a local historian, tells us, 'In about 1905 flour production ceased and the mill went over to animal feed production only. The mill ran as a pure watermill until the early 1960s when gradually electric power crept in until now only a pair of stones can be driven by the water wheel. However, on a few days in the year one can still smell the scent of freshly ground warm meal and hear the slap – slap – slap of the water wheel.'

⌘ STEEPLE

Architects tend to sneer at the church of St Lawrence and All Saints. It was rebuilt in 1884, on a new site, to the design of Frederick Chancellor, the Chelmsford-based architect. He used much of the material from the demolition of the old church, but mixed it up higgledy-piggledy with brown stone and bricks, in such a way that it looks absolutely charming, the sort of village church that expatriates have in mind when they dream of home.

Old and new houses are mixed haphazardly on the village street. This dichotomy is well illustrated by the story of the public house, the Sun and Anchor. It was built in 1940, probably the only such house to have been erected at that difficult time, simply because it was already under way. Very modern for that period, it stands in stark contrast to the old public house next door, which has since been divided into two handsome cottages named Sun and Anchor respectively. The old pub, originally the Anchor, was built in the 18th century and for more than 30 years the Spurgin family ran it. Susannah Spooner and her son Summerset ran it then as the Sun and Anchor. Christopher Chipps and his wife Ellen were the tenants of Grays, the Chelmsford brewers for 40 years from 1899, then their son Azel and his wife Victoria May took over and moved into the new Sun and Anchor.

The parish boundary to the north is the river Blackwater. A couple of narrow roads take the motorist up to glorious views down the estuary where the big power station is seen as a purple smudge on the horizon. But do not think you will be alone, walking the sea wall in glorious solitude; one road gives on to a holiday home and caravan park as well as the Steeple Sailing Club headquarters, while the other gives access not only to the vestigial remains of Stansgate Priory but also to the very lively premises of the Marconi Sailing Club.

⌘ STOCK

On the highest land in the village, the site of the Roman Catholic cemetery, there is faint evidence of a rampart and ditch defence system. One local expert has suggested that it could have been a stronghold of Queen Boadicea! He is on firmer ground when it comes to Roman occupation, for remains of their pottery were found in the same area in 1885. It was the Saxons who settled the place sufficiently to give it a name, which was written down in the register of property transactions, the 'Feet of Fines', as 'Herwardstoc' meaning 'outlying farmstead of a man called Hereweard'.

The church was first built by the Saxons; then, still using timber from the forest, it was rebuilt some 700 years ago – a miracle of construction, which can still be seen today in the way the four great posts of the belfry were set up, braced and strutted to take the weight of the bells under the tall slim spire. A land mine fell in the churchyard during the Second World War, but that construction held.

Inside one memorial stands out. It is a brass to Richard Twedye who died in 1574, showing him in full armour. He was a brave soldier and a local benefactor, as the inscription shows:

The village church at Stock

'Bewrapte in clay and so reserved until the Joyefull dome
Whoe in his lyffe hath served well against the Ingleshe foes
In fforen landes and eke at home his countrye well yt knowes
The prince he served in courte full longe, a pensioner fitt in personage
In his countrye a Justice eke, a man full grave and sage
Ffoure almeshowses here hath he builte for foure poore knights to dwell
And then indowed with stipend lardge enoughe to kepe them well . . .

Those four almshouses, restored and modernised can still be seen on the little green opposite the church. In the process of modernisation a remarkable discovery was made. Under the floor of one cottage were found three large pots, buried before the hearth in a circle with their necks touching in the middle. These pots were made around the time that a woman in Stock was declared to be a witch; Agnes Sawen, tried in 1576, had a year in prison at Colchester and was made to stand in the pillory in the market place for six hours every quarter while she confessed to her supposed sin.

⌘ TERLING

This must surely be one of the most unspoilt villages in the county. Much of the credit must go to the Strutt family for the excellent, sympathetic management of their property. On our visit we were told to pronounce Terling like darling. This is

Terling

a place to walk about. To the west, Gamble's Green is overlooked by the windmill, now a family home. Few people realise that it was originally designed not to produce flour but to grind bark; that was in 1818. It was later converted to corn grinding and was run by the Bonners, father and son. The old man aged 78 was on his own in the mill on 30th March 1950 when he became entangled in the cogs. His screams were heard by his son, but he died before he could be freed. The horrible coincidence is that this mill had been used in the comedy film, *Oh! Mr. Porter!* starring Will Hay, in which a man was whirled round on the sails.

The wide ford across the Ter as we approach the centre of the village has been the undoing of more than one over-confident motorist putting his car at it like a horse at a water jump. Then there is a pleasant journey past any number of beautifully kept old cottages and colour-washed houses as one makes for the church of All Saints. Among many other interesting features look for the unusual sundial high up on the red-brick tower of 1723.

Terling Place, home of the Strutts, is a beautiful late Georgian house. The central part was designed by John Johnson, the man who built Chelmsford's Shire Hall.

⌘ THAXTED

When you stand in the beautiful church, it is hard to imagine the cursing and swearing, the struggling and fighting which went on there on Friday, 24th September 1647. The trouble was that, as Puritanism swept the country at the onset of the Civil War, the vicar of Thaxted, Mr Newman Leader, was replaced by a Mr Hall. But Lady Maynard, who had the power to appoint the vicar, would not agree. She wanted Edmund Croxon, even though everybody said he was a drunken blackguard.

She would not budge, so a great crowd of Thaxted people escorted their man to church and had him preach the sermon. When they tried to repeat the performance in the afternoon, church officials barred their way. They were furious; they grabbed those officials, beat them up, and made them flee for their lives. But the townspeople lost the day; their ringleaders were rounded up and taken for trial before the House of Lords that very same day, which shows how important the government and the church thought this sign of unrest in Essex was.

Believe it or not, that scene was re-enacted in the same church in 1921. Lady Warwick, a Maynard before marriage, had chosen Conrad Noel as vicar. She was a committed socialist and he, grandson of the Earl of Gainsborough, was secretary of the Church Socialist League, so he had her full support. The trouble was that he went a bit too far in mixing communism with Christianity. High in the church, alongside the national flag of St George, he hung not only the flag of Sinn Fein but also the red flag of communism.

Cambridge undergraduates got to hear of it, came down to Thaxted in a body, tore down Noel's flags and put up the Union Jack. Noel's supporters ripped it down, burned it, and replaced their flags. The shouting and swearing which it engendered was repeated yet again on Empire Day of that year when one of Noel's followers had his hat knocked off for failing to remove it when the national anthem was played. The fighting spilled out into the streets and cars and motor bikes had their tyres slashed.

⌘ THORPE-LE-SOKEN

Two hundred and fifty years ago Thorpe, once described as a neat little town, was the setting for one of the most romantic stories to come out of Essex.

Kitty was born in 1720 to Robert Canham, a well-to-do farmer who lived in Beaumont Hall, to the east of Tendring. She grew up happily and made a good marriage with the Reverend Alexander Gough. It was not long, though, before Kitty was disillusioned with the humdrum of life in the vicarage. One day she just upped and left. She left not a word for her husband, changed her name so that she could not be traced and headed for London.

By the sheerest good luck she fell into good company and was introduced to Lord Dalmeny, son of the second Earl of Rosebery. He fell deeply in love with her and asked her to marry him. She just could not tell her guilty secret. She married him, and their honeymoon stretched on and on. For four years they wandered round Europe. Then, at Verona, Kitty became ill. When she realised that death was inevitable she scrawled a note which read, 'I am the wife of the Reverend Alexander Gough, vicar of Thorpe-le-Soken in Essex ... My last request is to be buried at Thorpe'.

That was in 1752, and amazing though it may seem, his Lordship carried out her wish to the letter. He had her body embalmed, packed it in a special case and set sail for England. At the graveside the two husbands stood side by side, united in their undying love for one woman.

There is still a rumour in this village that Sir William Gull, learned physician who attended the Prince of Wales was not buried in this churchyard as he should have been. His coffin was lowered into the grave, weighted with stones, while he was himself not dead at all, but locked away in a private madhouse, because he was Jack the Ripper!

⌘ TILTY

The abbey here, started by seven Cistercian monks in 1153, grew to buildings in stone, with a church built by 1221. By then a large community was tending vast flocks of sheep from which Tilty wool was harvested and exported throughout Europe because it was so fine. Then the Black Death broke out in the abbey, and so many brothers died that there were not enough survivors to run the large establishment. Following its closure by Henry VIII, its lands passed into secular hands. By 1542 Thomas Audley of Walden, the Lord Chancellor, had acquired the abbey. He tore it down to put up his own palace. In time that too crumbled away and was gradually carted off for other purposes.

The only part of the abbey left was the chapel at the gate, which the villagers had used as their parish church. That use was allowed to continue, the church was repaired through all this time and stands today. The huge beautiful east window, with its delicate tracery is quite out of proportion with the present building; it shows how splendid the abbey buildings must have been. The church was open when we visited it and we were able to see the glass case with a wide selection of finds, curious and archaeological, which have turned up on the site of the abbey in the meadow below the church, where one last wall remains.

During the war, when tobacco was scarce, the vicar said in his parish magazine that he would pass on his secrets of successful tobacco curing to anybody who would pay five shillings toward the restoration of Tilty tower. A daily paper spotted this, let it be known nationally and Hugh received sacks of letters enclosing the necessary fee. So we may frown on tobacco today, but it did preserve that tower for us and generations after us to enjoy.

⌘ TOLLESBURY

There is so much to see down by Woodrolfe creek: the old fishermen's lofts, now restored and put to new uses, the well-organised marina, the footpath which will

Tollesbury marina

take you down to the estuary where the 'Crab and Winkle' railway made its last stop on the quay to load up supplies for the famous jam-factory at Tiptree. But let us first stop by the church of St Mary in the centre of this large village.

The feature which must surely catch your eye is the font, a pretty little octagonal bowl upon a graceful stem. Upon it a message is inscribed in gothic letters: 'Good people all I pray take care, that in ye church you do not sware, As this man did'. A puzzling message which, fortunately, can be understood by reference to the church's register of baptisms, now kept in the Essex Record Office, under the 30th of August 1718:

'Elizabeth, daughter of Robert and Eliza Wood, being the first childe whom was baptised in the New Font which was bought out of five pounds paid by John Norman, who some months before came into the church and cursed and talked loud in the time of Divine service, to prevent his being prosecuted for which he paid by agreement the above said five pounds. Note that the wise rhymes on the font were put there by the sole order of Robert Joyce then churchwarden.'

⌘ TOLLESHUNT D'ARCY

Few places have the good fortune to be described lovingly by a famous author for the benefit of future generations. Margery Allingham, the well-known writer of detective stories, did just that for Tolleshunt D'Arcy.

The author, Margery Allingham, lived here in Tolleshunt D'Arcy

It was after her marriage to Philip Youngman Carter that she came to live in this village. The house they chose to live in, Georgian-fronted D'Arcy House, had been the home of the equally famous Doctor Salter. When her husband went off to war, Margery soon got involved in village affairs and carried on writing. An American friend asked her to put down what the daily life of country people in England was like during the Second World War. So she wrote *The Oaken Heart*, all about her time in Tolleshunt D'Arcy, though she actually called it Auburn.

There must be many an inhabitant today who remembers the old 'Crab and Winkle' railway from Kelvedon to Tollesbury which she described:

'It is a nice little train with a high-pitched tootle and a fearsome tendency to rock like a boat in the high winds from over the saltings ...'

Dr Salter, born in 1841, took up the local practice in 1864, when as he says in his diary, he was, 'Received with great cheering at the entrance to the village'. He loved his patients and they loved him. He was a robust character, who liked dogs and horses, and even went to Russia to judge their dog shows. He is now remembered for his diary, which included so much of the life of the locality. The original is now lost, but a shortened version was printed and is in most of the larger Essex libraries. He died in 1932 and his tombstone can still be seen in the extension of the village churchyard.

⌘ UGLEY

Every Women's Institute has its place-name before it – that is, every one except this village. After all, who would want to join Ugley Women's Institute? So, by special dispensation it is called the Women's Institute of Ugley. It is a pity that the Old English name for the settlement, 'Ugga's woodland clearing' is so misunderstood in modern times. It reminds us that the Saxon leader, Ugga, brought his family clan across the North Sea to start a new life in this verdant land, where they cut down the forest and put up their hall and their church – focal points of their daily lives. Those sites are still occupied by the later rebuildings of Ugley Hall and St Peter's church, under the limes which dwarf the old brick tower of 1550.

Wander the churchyard and read the tombstone to the Jordan boys, Walter and Harry, who went away from Ugley's rustic tranquillity to the First World War – and did not come back. There is a pleasant but demanding walk down the rough bridleway to Ugley Green a mile and a half away. The car driver has to go down to the old A11, now the B1383, and turn off east, passing Orford House, built by Admiral Russell just after he was made Earl of Orford around 1700.

The house was bought by the Home Farm Trust, beautifully restored and adapted to meet the needs of young handicapped people, who are thus enabled to live on their own, look after themselves and at the same time enjoy the company of friends. At the Green itself, the village pump still stands. Beside it is a great boulder

The village pump and pudding-stone at Ugley

of pudding-stone which was, no doubt, a signpost for prehistoric man, marking the track through the forest up the hill. Modern man rushes by on the M11 just a step to the east, unaware of what he is missing!

⌘ ULTING

Ulting is not a particularly picturesque village. It does not gather round its church because All Saints stands in what can only be called a field rather than a churchyard, running down the hill to the very bank of the Chelmer. It is the only church right on the bank throughout the course of that river. Its attractions are its diminutive size, its 13th century architecture and its setting in such a lush, overgrown, riverside meadow. Sad to say it is its very isolation which requires it to be kept locked against vandalism.

There may be many Essex folk who have not heard of Ulting, yet it has a very important place in the story of Essex. It is the site of the first sugar factory in Britain. Part of the river Chelmer in this parish is still called 'Sugar Baker's Holes'. The sugar was extracted from sugar beet, a process invented by a German in 1747. Napoleon developed it to beat the British blockade of cane-sugar from the West Indies. By 1816 the French had set up 213 factories. It was not until 1832 that Britain became interested, when our Essex firm of Marriage, Reid and Marriage set

Sugar Baker's Holes, Ulting

up a sugar mill. It was sited right by the river so that vast supplies of sugar beet could be brought in by barge.

Their enterprise was strangled by a drop in the price of cane sugar. The mill closed and was eventually demolished, but that was not the end of the story of sugar in Essex. A big new factory, using modern methods was established at Felsted in 1926. Then the wheel of fortune turned again. National eating habits veered away from sweet obesity, much less sugar was consumed and so that factory also closed.

⌘ WALTHAM ABBEY

A precious document, written more than 800 years ago and kept in the British Museum tells the strange story of the building of Waltham Abbey somewhere around 1030. A blacksmith at Montacute in Somerset was told in a dream to get the priest and the villagers to dig in the hill above the village and they would find treasure. They dug, and they found deep in the ground a huge stone cleft in two; inside was an image of Christ on the cross, all carved out in black flint. The local lord and landowner, Tovi le Prude, knew that this was a sign from God. He hoisted the cross on to a waggon and harnessed to it twelve red oxen and twelve white cows. He said they would go wherever God willed, and prayed for guidance.

The beautiful interior of Waltham Abbey

He mentioned one holy place of pilgrimage after another, from Glastonbury to Winchester, but the animals would not move.

Then he thought of the little settlement in the woods in Essex called Waltham, where he was having a country house built. He said its name – and the waggon moved. All those miles the waggon rolled, stopping while men and animals were refreshed, then pressing on remorselessly until it came to Waltham and stopped for the last time.

Even as the cross was consecrated, the great crowd that had gathered and followed it for miles saw blood flow symbolically from that flint image of Christ. Tovi was so overcome by it all that he gave his entire wealth to the founding of communities of the Holy Cross in Waltham, Kelvedon, Loughton and Alverton, which is probably the Alderton Hall of today.

Eventually ownership of the land passed into the hands of Earl Harold and the building of a magnificent church was put in hand. What the visitor will see there today is the rebuilding of 1242, with later additions.

⌘ WALTON-ON-THE-NAZE

'Miles of clean, sandy beaches – ideal for paddling, bathing and building sandcastles; exciting cliffs with acres of grassy play area at their summit ...' – the district guide is absolutely right; these are the features our family has enjoyed over the years. There is more to it than that. For instance, the very long pier takes us out into the North Sea where we can look back and ponder on the reason for the tower which pokes up high almost due north. The answer is that the tower has no other purpose than to act as a landmark, put up on the Naze by Trinity House back in 1720. It guided shipping to the busy port of Harwich, and many a smuggler was grateful for it, silhouetted against the night sky, as he made for Hamford Water and the creeks that led far inland.

The real old village of Walton is now some nine miles out to sea, on the West Rocks. Its church finally fell into the sea in 1798. The new town grew from the early 19th century fad for sea bathing as a way to good health. Marine Parade was the first street completed, called then The Crescent. Now Walton has a very good shopping centre and all the amusements and recreation delights associated with the seaside.

The Naze is a marvellous, wild, grass-covered open space on the cliff which can swallow up crowds of people and still provide peaceful walks and picnics for family groups. Where the sea has eroded the cliffs below the Naze there is a particular geological deposit of earth known as the Red Crag; in it fossils of all kinds can be found, from the shark's teeth to the whale's ear bone shown in the Chelmsford and Essex Museum.

⌘ WITHAM

When Witham's bypass opened on 15th September 1964, the town could breathe again, shoppers could actually cross the road. Since then the place has been expanded, with London overspill people finding homes on the new estates and jobs in the new industries which have taken up sites reaching right out to the bypass. Some 700 years ago, the Knights Templar, with headquarters at Cressing, owned the land here. Then the town centre was Chipping Hill – a 'cheaping' was a market – but the Knights saw the advantages of setting up trade on the rapidly developing highway down by the bridge across the river Brain.

Between those ancient and modern developments there was yet another scheme of expansion, promoted in 1737. Dr Taverner rediscovered a chalybeate spring just outside Witham. He aimed to make it the centre of a spa, with Witham becoming a second Tunbridge Wells. To this end he wrote a prospectus and had it circulated. Owners of properties all down the main street had new frontages put on their businesses to impress the promised flood of customers.

The spa, however, did not take off; Witham metaphorically shrugged its shoulders and settled back again as a small market town and shopping centre. And that is what it is today. Nearby is the parish church of St Nicholas with two lovely surprises inside. One is the 15th century carved wooden rood screen with the cross still in position. The other is the altar tomb on which life-size effigies of John Southcote, a judge of the Queen's bench who died in 1585, and his wife are shown in their best dress in full colour.

⌘ WOODHAM MORTIMER

This is a place which motorists rush through on their way to Maldon from the west, unaware that one of the world's most useful inventions was conceived here – the forceps, used to help in cases of difficult childbirth.

Peter Chamberlen, born in 1601, was a 'man-midwife', as he was then called, of some importance. He followed his uncle as Physician Extraordinary to Charles I and II. He kept out of the turmoil of the Civil War by buying Woodham Mortimer Hall out in the country, but still within a day's ride of his practice in London. Here he brought up a family of 18 children. His great success was due to his use of the forceps he had invented. He delivered children safely where, before, lingering labour had often led to the death of mother and baby. He would not allow other people into the room to see the way he worked. For 100 years, succeeding generations of Chamberlen doctors achieved fame and fortune by the deft use of forceps, until, early in the 18th century, an impecunious Chamberlen sold the secret to a Dutch surgeon, who had them made for sale to the profession. In 1813, the owner of the Hall found under a loose floorboard a wooden box containing Peter Chamberlen's original forceps! Chamberlen's body lies in the north east corner of the churchyard.

In the field on the other side of the road from the church, a little square of railing protects an obelisk, on which is written, 'In grateful remembrance of the munificent bequest by William Alexander Esqr. of his estate at Woodham Mortimer in the County of Essex for the benefit, behoof and advantage of the poor of the Company of Coopers, London, for ever, the master, wardens and court of assistants of the company have erected this memorial not only as a tribute of their respect and admiration but also with a view of publickly handing down to future ages so splendid an act of disinterested generosity, 1825.'

William Alexander was born around 1673. Apprenticed to a cooper, he served a seven-year term until, in 1697, he was admitted to the Company as a fully-fledged cooper and set up his own business. He did so well that he was able to buy Woodham Mortimer Hall in its 300 acres of land and lease it out to a farmer.

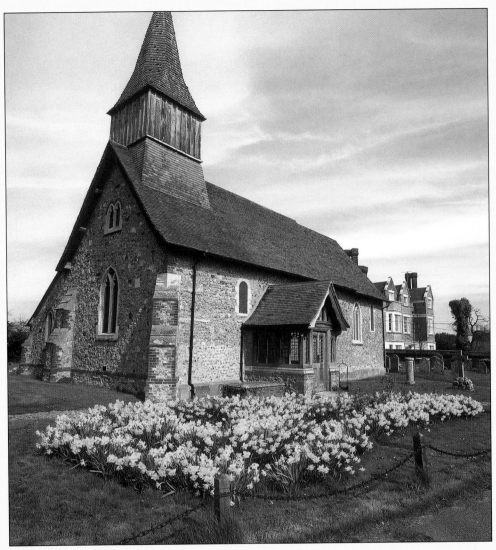

St Margaret's church, Woodham Mortimer

⌘ WRITTLE

The College of Agriculture stands on the site of a hunting lodge built for King John in 1211. It makes no fuss about this, after all there are so many points of historical interest in this village that justice cannot be done to them all in a short space. The most interesting book written about Writtle never went into print, but there is a copy kept in the Chelmsford library.

It was compiled by young students backed by Toc H and C.P.R.E. They came in

The historic village of Writtle

July 1965 and camped out on the village green, and they went round asking questions and writing like fury. They found the Roman bricks in the church walls and went on to William the Conqueror taking over the Lordship of Writtle from the ousted Harold. They traced the connection of Robert the Bruce with the village and showed how Writtle was granted by Queen Mary to the Petre family of Ingatestone.

They inspected the two village greens, the three pleasant pubs and the fine parish church and they lighted on the entrance at the far end of St John's Green, to what was then the research establishment of Marconi's, the wireless engineers and manufacturers. It was from this corner of the world that the first public wireless transmission was sent out to a marvelling public on 14th February 1922.